SIMPLE, DELICIOUS RECIPES
FOR CLASSIC LATIN AMERICAN FLAVORS

T0356000

AUTHENTIC BRAZILIAN
HOME COOKING

OLIVIA MESQUITA
CREATOR OF OLIVIA'S CUISINE

PAGE STREET
PUBLISHING CO.

DEDICATION

To Manuda, my grandma, the love of my life.

CONTENTS

INTRODUCTION

Hi! My name is Olivia Mesquita, and I'm a Brazilian expat, born and raised in São Paulo, who immigrated to the United States almost 13 years ago, all starry-eyed and ready to pursue a career on Broadway. Somewhere along the way, I fell out of love with acting (or more specifically, the soul-crushing hustle of an acting career in NYC) and discovered my passion for cooking and sharing recipes with the world. And that's how, in 2014, my blog Olivia's Cuisine was born.

Like most Brazilians who choose to leave Brazil, I eventually felt homesick and found comfort in cooking recipes that I grew up eating, which also meant countless video and phone calls to my grandmother so she could teach me her recipes.

Growing up, my grandmother didn't just teach me how to cook, she taught me how to eat! Not the mechanical, physical act of eating, of course, but how to enjoy and value delicious home-cooked meals that were prepared with love. Nothing my grandmother served ever tasted anything less than a meal from a five-star restaurant, and I'm 100 percent certain it was because she imbued lots of love in everything she cooked.

Because of her, I grew up with the belief that food is way more than nutrition. It is an expression of one's self, including culture, values and—especially—emotions! Nothing says "I love you" like a home-cooked meal, and few things feel as rewarding as friends and family excitedly gathering around the table to eat something you've prepared for them.

When I started my blog, it was simply a way to express myself and share recipes that were special to me. I never went to culinary school. I jumped in fear every time I tried to flambé anything and always made my husband stand nearby with a fire extinguisher. (He still likes to do that.) I didn't even own a good chef's knife, let alone any special cookware or appliances. The passion for food and cooking was there; the skills and confidence (and fancy tools) eventually followed!

At first, my website was dedicated to sharing family recipes, from Brazilian classics to the Italian and Lebanese dishes that are a strong part of our cuisine in the Southeastern part of the country where I'm from. With time, it became a place to document and share my cooking journey, either by cooking dishes that were near and dear to my heart—such as my grandma's Estrogonofe de Carne (Beef Stroganoff; page 11) and her Pavê da Manuda (Manuda's Trifle; page 140)—or by recreating something I've tasted on a trip or at a restaurant.

When the opportunity to write a Brazilian cookbook presented itself, I eagerly grabbed it! I am beyond honored to be chosen to represent our cuisine, and I dream of a world with more Brazilian restaurants and more of our ingredients available at local grocery stores all over the world.

If you are a Brazilian living abroad, I hope my recipes bring you a taste of home and that they help you cook our comidinha with ingredients available near you. And if you're not Brazilian and are just interested in Brazilian food and cooking, I am excited to have you try not only some of our classic dishes but some you haven't ever heard of before. Little by little, the world will see us as more than soccer and samba, and our cuisine is a great place to start!

Olivia Mesquita

CARNES

Rice and beans might be the heart and soul of Brazilian cuisine, but meat and fish give it personality. Proteins from animal sources go way beyond steak for churrasco, and our cuisine uses of a variety of beef, chicken, pork and fish to create our traditional recipes.

Depending on the region, you will see one protein shining brighter than the other, with fish being favored in the North—in dishes such as Peixada à Baiana (Fish Stew in Coconut Milk; page 52)—and beef heavily consumed in the South, where dishes like Barreado na Panela de Pressão (Instant Pot Cumin Beef Stew; page 23) and Filé à Oswaldo Aranha (Filet Mignon with Garlic; page 31) are beloved!

I have, of course, included a couple of recipes that use picanha, such as Picanha no Forno com Manteiga de Alho (Oven-Roasted Picanha with Garlic Butter) on page 24 and Hambúrguer de Picanha com Maionese Verde (Picanha Burger with Green Milk Mayo) on page 27, since it's the most famous cut of beef in Brazil and always a hit among meat lovers. If you want to impress some carnivore friends, picanha is the way to go!

BEEF

YIELD: 6 SERVINGS

2 lb (907 g) tenderloin, sirloin, boneless rib eye or strip steak, cut into small cubes

Kosher salt and freshly ground black pepper, as desired

1 tbsp (7 g) sweet paprika

1 tbsp (8 g) all-purpose flour

2 tbsp + 1 tsp (35 ml) olive oil, divided

2 tbsp (28 g) unsalted butter

2 medium onions, grated

¼ cup (60 ml) cognac or brandy (optional)

1 tbsp (15 ml) Dijon mustard

2 tbsp (30 ml) ketchup

2 tbsp (30 ml) Worcestershire sauce

1 (14-oz [397-g]) can peeled tomatoes, blended until smooth

1 (6-oz [170-g]) jar of sliced mushrooms, drained (see Notes)

1 cup (240 ml) heavy cream

Rice, for serving

Shoestring fries (batata palha), for serving

ESTROGONOFE DE CARNE
(BEEF STROGANOFF)

The first recipe in this book had to be the most special one: my grandma's beef stroganoff. Everybody has a family recipe that makes their heart swell with love every time they eat it, and this is mine. Whenever I make it, it's like I can feel her there in the kitchen with me, bringing me up to date with the latest family gossip.

If you haven't tried Brazilian-style stroganoff, you might turn your nose up at some of the ingredients, which are different than the ones used in traditional Russian stroganoff. Ketchup? Heavy cream instead of sour cream? Yep. You'll just have to trust me here, as—in my humble opinion—this is the best stroganoff you will ever taste!

Combine the cubed steak, salt, pepper, paprika and flour in a bowl, tossing well so all the beef pieces are thoroughly coated. Reserve.

Heat 1 teaspoon (5 ml) of the olive oil and the butter in a large skillet or sauté pan over medium heat. Stir in the onions and cook for 3 to 5 minutes, or until the onions absorb the butter and their color turns from white to golden. Remove to a bowl and reserve. Add the remaining olive oil to the skillet and turn the heat to medium-high. Once shimmering, add the beef, working in batches if necessary, and cook for 5 minutes, or until browned. Add the cognac, if using, and deglaze the pan, using a wooden spoon to scrape all the browned bits from the bottom of the pan. Then, let it cook for 3 minutes, or until the liquid has evaporated.

Return the onions to the skillet, and add the mustard, ketchup, Worcestershire sauce, blended tomatoes and a pinch of salt and pepper. Bring it to a boil, and then lower the heat to medium-low, cover and simmer for 10 minutes. Stir in the mushrooms and cook for 5 minutes. Pour in the heavy cream and cook for 5 to 10 minutes, or until the sauce thickens slightly. Taste and adjust the seasoning as needed. Serve immediately with rice and shoestring fries (batata palha).

NOTES
I have tried to keep this recipe as close to the original as possible. My grandma always used what we Brazilians call champignons, or preserved mushrooms in a jar, which is why I call for a jar of sliced mushrooms. I confess I almost always use fresh instead, which I sauté in butter in another pan before adding to the stroganoff.

2 tbsp (30 ml) olive oil

1 large onion, finely chopped

4 cloves garlic, finely minced

2 lb (907 g) carne seca (page 15), desalted, cooked and shredded

2 Roma tomatoes, finely diced

Kosher salt and freshly ground black pepper, as desired

⅓ cup (21 g) chopped parsley

3 lb (1.5 kg) peeled yuca, root removed and cut into 2" (5-cm) chunks (see Notes)

ESCONDIDINHO DE CARNE SECA

(BRAZILIAN COTTAGE PIE)

Escondidinho is a classic Brazilian casserole dish, popular all over the country. It can be made with various types of protein, such as carne seca, ground beef, chicken, turkey, fish, seafood, and different kinds of mashed roots, such as yuca, potatoes or even pumpkin. I like to think of it as the tropical version of a cottage (shepherd's) pie!

The name escondidinho comes from the meat being hidden (escondida) under the mashed root, almost like a prize for those who dig in! This is a great casserole to throw together whenever you are craving comfort food. You can serve it as is with some crusty bread or serve with rice. And, if you're strapped for time, it can be made 1 or 2 days ahead and baked when you plan on serving it!

In a large skillet, heat the olive oil over medium heat and sauté the onion for 3 to 5 minutes, or until translucent. Add the garlic and cook for 1 minute, or until fragrant and no longer raw. Stir in the carne seca, letting it cook for 2 to 3 minutes so it can absorb the flavors from the aromatics. Then add the tomatoes and cook for 3 to 5 minutes, or until they have softened. Taste before seasoning with salt and pepper. Stir in the parsley and reserve.

Preheat the oven to 450°F (230°C).

Place the yuca chunks in a large saucepan and add enough water to cover them completely, along with a pinch of salt. Cook over medium-high heat, until it starts to boil, then lower the heat to medium-low and cook for 20 to 30 minutes, or until the yuca is very tender. (You can also cook the yuca for 15 minutes in a pressure cooker.) Drain and let dry for a couple of minutes so any extra moisture can evaporate.

(continued)

1 cup (240 ml) heavy cream

1 cup (100 g) freshly grated Parmesan cheese, divided

1 cup (112 g) shredded low-moisture mozzarella

ESCONDIDINHO DE CARNE SECA
(CONTINUED)

Warm the heavy cream in the microwave for 30 seconds. While the yuca is still hot, mash the yuca with a potato masher, ricer, immersion blender or a good ol' fork. Return the mashed yuca to the pot—which should still be hot—and gradually stir in the warm cream. Add ½ cup (56 g) of the Parmesan and season with salt and pepper.

To assemble the escondidinho, add half of the mashed yuca to the bottom of a baking dish that has been greased with oil or nonstick spray (see Notes), then layer all of the carne seca mixture, followed by the remaining mashed yuca. Top with the mozzarella cheese and remaining Parmesan. Bake for 20 to 30 minutes, or until bubbly and golden brown. Remove from the oven and let it cool for a few minutes before serving.

NOTES

- *Peeling yuca can be intimidating, since its skin is so hard. However, if you use a sharp chef's knife and work in smaller chunks, you have nothing to fear. To peel it, start by cutting the ends of the root and cutting it into smaller 2- to 3-inch (5- to 8-cm) segments. Stand each piece up with the flat end down, and then use the sharp knife to cut away the skin vertically until it has been completely peeled off. Keep rotating and slicing away the skin until the whole root is peeled. To cut off the core, just slice the peeled yuca in half lengthwise to expose the woody core, then cut it lengthwise again so that the yuca is now quartered with the core exposed. Stand each piece and use the knife to cut the core off.*

- *Escondidinho can also be assembled as individual portions in ramekins or individual cast-iron skillets or bowls.*

CARNE SECA

Carne seca is beef (cuts vary) that goes through a salting process followed by dehydration for longer preservation. You will also find it by the name charque or carne de sol; however, even though these names can be used interchangeably, there are differences in their preparation. You can find carne seca or carne de sol at Brazilian grocery stores or online. Do not use American beef jerky or Mexican machaca de res, as they will not work the same way.

Before you use carne seca in this and other recipes in this book, you will have to desalt it and—sometimes—cook it and shred it beforehand.

DESALT CARNE SECA

To desalt the carne seca, you can choose between two methods: the traditional, lengthy one, or the quick one, for those of us, like me, who are not good at planning ahead.

Traditional Method: Cut the carne seca into 1- to 2-inch (2.5- to 5-cm)-wide cubes and place in a bowl. Cover with water, then cover the bowl with plastic wrap and refrigerate for 12 hours. During these 12 hours, drain and replace the water at least three times. Finally, drain and cook the carne seca before using it in a recipe.

Quick Method: Rinse the carne seca well to get rid of any surface salt. Cut the carne seca in cubes, then place in a large pot (or pressure cooker if that's what you're using to cook it). Cover with water and bring to a boil. Cook for 10 minutes, and then drain and replace the water. Bring to a boil again and repeat the process two or three more times. You will know it's ready when you taste a small piece and it tastes salty but not overwhelmingly so.

COOKING CARNE SECA

To cook the carne seca, you can choose either to use a pressure cooker or the stove.

Pressure Cooker: Place the desalted carne seca in the pressure cooker and cover with water. Cook on high pressure for 40 minutes, with a 10-minute natural release. Drain, then shred (if needed) and use as directed in the recipe.

Stovetop: Place the carne seca in a saucepan and cover with water. Cook, over medium-high heat, until boiling. Lower the heat to a simmer and cook for 1 to 3 hours, or as long as it takes for it to get tender.

2½ lb (1.1 kg) chuck roast

Kosher salt and freshly ground black pepper, as desired

1 tbsp (15 ml) vegetable oil

2 large yellow onions, peeled and sliced

4 cloves garlic, minced

½ cup (120 ml) red wine

1 tbsp (16 g) tomato paste

1 tbsp (14 g) brown sugar

1 (14-oz [397-g]) can crushed tomatoes

2 tbsp (30 ml) Worcestershire sauce

1 cup (240 ml) beef stock (½ cup [120 ml] for Instant Pot Method)

1 bay leaf

2 red bell peppers

CARNE LOUCA
(BRAISED BEEF WITH ONIONS, TOMATO AND PEPPERS)

Carne Louca—which translates to "crazy meat"—is a Brazilian childhood classic! It's a must at children's birthday parties or family gatherings and is usually served in bread rolls. It's tender, shredded beef cooked with onions, peppers and a touch of vinegar to brighten everything up! Some people like adding olives and/or capers and while I haven't included them in the recipe, you can certainly do that if desired. I am including the method for both stovetop and Instant Pot versions, for your convenience.

I have no idea why this dish has this name, but I have a feeling it's because it is crazy good.

Stovetop Method

Season the chuck roast generously with salt and pepper, and cut into three parts. That will make it easier to sear in the pot. Heat the oil in a large Dutch oven or heavy-bottomed pot over medium-high heat, until hot and shimmering. Sear the beef pieces on all sides for 5 to 8 minutes, or until nice and brown all over. Remove to a plate and reserve.

Reduce the heat to medium. Add the onions with a pinch of salt, and sauté for 3 minutes, or until softened. Stir in the garlic and cook for 1 minute so it's no longer raw. Pour in the red wine, using a wooden spoon to scrape all the browned bits from the bottom of the pot. Cook for 2 minutes, or until the wine has evaporated. Stir in the tomato paste and brown sugar. Then, add the crushed tomatoes, Worcestershire sauce, beef stock and bay leaf. Season with salt and pepper. Bring to a boil, and then return the beef and its juices to the pot. Cover, reduce the heat to low and simmer for 2½ hours, or until fall-apart tender.

While the beef is cooking, roast the peppers on a gas stove or in the oven under the broiler. To do so on the stove, turn the gas burner on high heat and lay the pepper directly on the flame. As the skin starts to burn, using kitchen tongs, rotate the pepper so all sides get blackened evenly. To char them in the oven, turn your broiler on and place the peppers in a baking sheet, 4 to 6 inches (10 to 15 cm) away from the heat source. Broil, flipping as they blacken, until they're blackened all over. Wrap the charred peppers in foil and let them sit for at least 15 minutes. The steam will soften them, making it easy to peel them. Unwrap the foil and use your fingers to pull off the blackened skins, discarding them. Remove seeds and stems, then thinly slice the peppers. Reserve.

(continued)

2 tsp (10 ml) balsamic vinegar

⅓ cup (21 g) chopped parsley

2 green onions, chopped

French bread or sandwich rolls, for serving

CARNE LOUCA
(CONTINUED)

Once the beef is tender, shred using two forks. Stir in the vinegar and peppers. If needed, turn the heat to medium-high and cook to reduce the sauce; the sauce should be on the thick side and not liquid-y like in a stew. Remove the bay leaf. Taste and adjust seasoning as needed. Stir in the parsley and green onions. Serve immediately, with pão francês (French bread) or sandwich rolls, or refrigerate (after it has cooled completely) for up to 2 days. Like most braised dishes, Carne Louca tastes even better the next day after the flavors have a chance to marry and become more pronounced.

Instant Pot Method

Season the chuck roast generously with salt and pepper, and cut into three parts. That will make it easier to sear in the Instant Pot. Set a 6-quart (6-L) or larger Instant Pot to sauté mode. Once hot, add the oil and the beef pieces. Sear on all sides until nice and brown all over, 2 minutes per side. Remove to a plate and reserve.

Add the onions with a pinch of salt, and sauté for 5 minutes, or until softened. Stir in the garlic and cook for 1 minute so it's no longer raw. Pour in the red wine, and use a wooden spoon to scrape all the browned bits from the bottom of the pot. Cook for 5 to 8 minutes, or until the liquid has evaporated. Stir in the tomato paste and brown sugar. Then, add the crushed tomatoes, Worcestershire sauce, ½ cup (100 ml) of the beef stock and bay leaf. Season with salt and pepper. Bring to a boil, then return the beef and its juices to the pot. Cover and select Pressure Cook or Manual, setting it to cook under high pressure for 50 minutes. Make sure the venting knob is at the sealing position. The timer won't start until there is enough pressure inside the pot, so it might take a while.

While the beef is cooking, prep the red bell peppers according to the directions under the Stovetop Method. Reserve. When the cooking time is up, let the pressure naturally release for 10 minutes, then carefully release the remaining pressure by turning the venting knob from sealing to venting. Remove the bay leaf. Shred using two forks, and then stir in the vinegar and peppers. If needed, turn the sauté function on and cook to reduce the sauce. The sauce should be on the thick side, not liquid-y like in a stew. Taste and adjust seasoning as needed. Stir in the chopped parsley and green onions. Serve immediately, with pão francês or sandwich rolls, or refrigerate (after it has cooled completely) for up to 2 days.

FOR THE SAUCE

1 (28-oz [794-g]) can peeled tomatoes, blended until smooth

¼ cup (57 g) unsalted butter

1 large onion, peeled and halved

Kosher salt and freshly ground black pepper, as desired

FOR THE STEAKS

2 (1-lb [454-g]) thin sirloin steaks (see Notes)

Kosher salt and freshly ground black pepper, as desired

1 cup (125 g) all-purpose flour

2 large eggs, beaten

2 cups (216 g) plain breadcrumbs

FILÉ À PARMIGIANA
(FILET PARMIGIANA)

You won't find filet or steak Parmigiana anywhere in Italy, as Italians make this dish with eggplant. This beef version is a Brazilian creation, specifically from the state of São Paulo, which has one of the largest Italian communities outside of Italy. This dish is so popular that São Paulo has whole restaurants devoted to it, such as the famous Bar do Alemão in Itú, or Restaurante Planeta's in São Paulo. Making it at home is a bit of a labor of love but so worth it! Yes, there's a bit of breading and frying involved, which always causes a bit of a mess, but at the end you'll be rewarded with one of my favorite dishes ever: succulent fried, breaded steaks topped with a simple-yet-flavorful silky tomato sauce and an ooey-gooey layer of not only one, but two types of cheese.

Don't even think about serving this over pasta, like you would eggplant or chicken Parmigiana. There is only one acceptable way to serve this, and it's with white rice and French fries, just like they do at the cantinas in São Paulo!

To make the sauce, in a large saucepan, combine the tomatoes, butter and onion halves. Cook over medium heat until it starts to boil. Cover and lower the heat, simmering for 15 to 20 minutes while you prepare the steaks. Discard the onion halves and season with salt and pepper. Reserve.

To make the steaks, generously season the steaks with salt and pepper. Place the flour in a large bowl and add a pinch of salt. In another bowl, lightly whisk the eggs with some salt and pepper. Place the breadcrumbs in a third bowl, seasoning generously with salt and pepper. Dredge the steaks in flour until coated, shaking off the excess flour. Then, dip them in the eggs, lifting them to let the excess egg drip off before coating in breadcrumbs. Use your hand to firmly press the breadcrumbs onto the steak to make sure they stick. Arrange the breaded steaks onto a large baking sheet lined with parchment paper. Refrigerate for 30 minutes.

Preheat the oven to 425°F (220°C) with a rack in the middle.

(continued)

Vegetable oil, for frying

1 clove garlic (see Notes)

8 oz (226 g) shredded low-moisture mozzarella

1 cup (100 g) shredded Parmesan cheese

FOR SERVING

Rice

French fries

FILÉ À PARMIGIANA
(CONTINUED)

Add oil and the garlic to a cast-iron skillet over medium-high heat. Once the garlic begins to fry, or when the oil reaches a temperature between 350 to 375°F (180 to 190°C), it is time to add the steaks. You can cook one at a time if needed, as you shouldn't overcrowd the pan. Fry on both sides for 2 to 3 minutes, or until golden brown. Then remove to a wire rack over a plate covered with paper towels to catch any excess grease. Place the fried steaks back on the baking sheet and cover them with the shredded mozzarella. Transfer to the oven and bake for 5 to 8 minutes, or until the cheese melts. Remove from oven and set aside.

In a large baking dish, spoon a layer of the sauce, then arrange the cheese-covered steaks on top of the sauce. Cover with the remaining sauce and top with the Parmesan. Place in the oven for 5 minutes, or until the Parmesan melts. Serve immediately with rice and French fries!

NOTES

- *I usually find already-pounded sirloin steaks at the meat aisle in my grocery store. If you can't find it, ask your butcher to do it for you or just pound them yourself at home.*

- *Adding garlic to the frying oil adds a subtle-yet-delicious garlic flavor to the breaded steaks. It's also a good way to tell when the oil is hot enough, as the garlic will start vigorously frying when it's time to fry the steaks. It's a trick I learned with my grandma that I always use whenever I'm frying something savory!*

3½ lb (1.6 kg) chuck roast, excess fat trimmed and cut into 1½–2" (4–5-cm) cubes

Kosher salt and freshly ground black pepper, as desired

1–2 tsp (2–4 g) ground cumin, or as desired

2 tbsp (30 ml) red wine vinegar

2 large onions, sliced

4 Roma tomatoes, cored and sliced

10 cloves garlic, minced

½ cup (30 g) chopped parsley

3 green onions, thinly sliced

1 tsp vegetable oil

8 oz (226 g) thick bacon, finely diced

3 bay leaves

1 qt (960 ml) water

Rice, for serving

Farofa, for serving (see Notes)

Sliced bananas, for serving

BARREADO NA PANELA DE PRESSÃO

(INSTANT POT CUMIN BEEF STEW)

This hearty beef stew is a staple in Paraná, a state in southern Brazil. There, it is considered a tradition to serve this stew during Carnaval along with a dose (or a few doses) of cachaça (Brazil's most popular spirit made from fermented surgarcane juice). After all, there's nothing like a nice, warm stew to give you the energy needed to dance and party for four consecutive days!

This dish was traditionally prepared in heavy clay cauldrons and cooked in a wood-fired stove for almost 24 hours. The name *barreado,* which comes from the word *barro (clay* in English) comes from the fact that the pot would have to be sealed (barreada) with a paste made of manioc flour and water. My version is a modern take on this classic dish, as we will use an Instant Pot instead of the clay pot and wood oven. Thanks to the pressure cooker, you can have this comforting meal on the table in two and a half hours instead of having to wait a whole day to enjoy it.

In a large bowl, combine the chuck pieces with the salt, pepper, cumin and red wine vinegar. Mix well, using your hands, so all the beef pieces are coated with the seasoning. Reserve. In a second bowl, combine the onions, tomatoes, garlic, parsley and green onions. Give everything a good stir, and then reserve.

Turn your Instant Pot on and set it to sauté. Do not wait for the pot to say it's hot. Drizzle the oil on the bottom of the pot, and then add the bacon, forming the bottom layer. Add half of the beef on top of that, followed by a layer of the veggies, another layer of beef and a final layer of veggies. Add the bay leaves and pour in the water, making sure it's enough to cover everything and that it doesn't go past the max line. Close the pot and cook at high pressure for 2 hours, with a natural release of 10 minutes. Then, quickly release any remaining pressure and open the lid. The beef will be so tender that you can shred it just by stirring with a wooden spoon, or—my favorite method—by pressing everything with a potato masher. Barreado is a soupy stew, but, if desired, you can set the Instant Pot back to sauté mode and let the stew boil to reduce the liquid. Remove the bay leaves, then taste and adjust seasoning as needed. Serve immediately (or the day after, as it tastes even better after a night in the fridge), with rice, farofa and sliced bananas.

NOTES
Farofa is a popular Brazilian side dish that consists of toasted manioc/cassava flour (farinha de mandioca) that is cooked with aromatics and various ingredients.

8 cloves garlic

⅓ cup (80 ml) olive oil, divided

Kosher salt and freshly ground black pepper, as desired

¼ cup (57 g) unsalted butter, softened

1 (3½-lb [1.6-kg]) piece picanha (see Notes)

8 Yukon Gold potatoes, quartered

3 red onions, peeled and quartered

4 thyme sprigs

NOTES

Picanha, Brazil's most beloved cut of beef, comes from rump cap muscle of the cattle. Recently, I have seen it sold as picanha at some grocery stores here in the U.S. as it gains popularity internationally. That being said, if your butcher doesn't know what it is, ask for rump cap or top sirloin cap and make sure to ask them to keep the fat cap on.

PICANHA NO FORNO COM MANTEIGA DE ALHO
(OVEN-ROASTED PICANHA WITH GARLIC BUTTER)

Who doesn't love picanha, the star of any Brazilian steakhouse? Well, in this version, you get to prepare it at home and cook it in your oven in under one hour. You're welcome!

You will notice that I call for the picanha to be cooked a little less than medium, as it gets quite chewy or rubbery when it's well done. If that's how you like your meat, go ahead and cook the hell out of it! If you, however, are looking for that perfect pink-medium doneness (or even a hardcore carnivore red), make sure to use a meat thermometer to check and don't let your picanha cook any hotter than 135°F (57°C), as its temperature will continue rising while it rests.

The vegetables not only work as a "rack" so the picanha doesn't touch the bottom of the dish—as that would lead to it being unevenly cooked and possibly overcooked—but also as a side dish! I also recommend some farofa (such as Viradinho de Couve on page 73) as an accompaniment.

Preheat the oven to 400°F (200°C).

Using a mortar and pestle, combine the garlic, 1 tablespoon (30 ml) of the olive oil and a pinch of salt. Grind until smooth, and then stir in the butter and some black pepper. Use a sharp thin knife to make some slits on the roast. Rub the garlic butter generously all over the roast, and then season with more salt and pepper. Reserve.

Cook the potatoes in a large pot with salted water for 8 to 10 minutes, or until they begin to soften but are not quite tender yet. Drain and arrange the potatoes, onions and thyme sprigs in a 9 x 13–inch (22 x 33–cm) or larger baking dish. Toss the vegetables with the remaining oil and season with salt and pepper. Arrange the prepared picanha, fat side up, on top of the veggies, using them as a "rack," and roast for 45 minutes, or until a kitchen thermometer inserted on the picanha's thickest part reads 130°F (54°C). Remove the picanha to rest for 10 minutes, then return the veggies to the oven if they are not quite done. You can also pop them under the broiler if they are cooked but need some more color or crispness. Slice the picanha against the grain and serve with the vegetables!

FOR THE GREEN MAYO

1 cup (240 ml) cold whole milk

2 cloves garlic

2 green onions

1 cup (60 g) fresh parsley

1 tbsp (15 ml) Dijon mustard

1 tbsp (15 ml) Worcestershire sauce

Juice of 1 lime

Kosher salt and freshly ground black pepper, as desired

2 cups (480 ml) vegetable or canola oil, or as needed

FOR THE BURGERS

2 lb (907 g) ground picanha (see Notes)

Kosher salt and freshly ground black pepper, as desired

6 slices cheddar (or your favorite) cheese

6 burger buns, toasted

Lettuce, tomato and sliced onions, for serving (optional)

HAMBÚRGUER DE PICANHA COM MAIONESE VERDE
(PICANHA BURGER WITH GREEN MILK MAYO)

If you've been to a hamburgueria (burger shop) in Brazil, chances are you've seen picanha burgers on the menu. Brazilians love picanha, so it's no surprise that we also use it to make burgers! This burger is almost always served with a special green mayo, made of milk and herbs, so I'm including a recipe for that too. The secret here is to use very cold milk to make the mayo. The colder the milk, the less oil you will need to emulsify it.

To make the green milk mayo: In a blender, combine the milk, garlic, green onions, parsley, Dijon mustard, Worcestershire sauce and lime juice. Season with salt and pepper. Blend until everything is incorporated and the mixture is green and foamy. Run the blender continuously on low and start very slowly pouring in the vegetable oil. Keep pouring the oil as a thin stream until the mayo thickens to a soft mayonnaise consistency. You might need less or more oil. Taste and adjust seasoning as needed. Refrigerate to set for at least 2 hours or up to 1 week.

To make the burgers, divide the ground meat into six equal portions, 5 ounces (142 g) each. Form the patties, without overworking the meat, making a thumbprint indentation into each patty. Aim for a ¾- to 1-inch (2- to 2.5-cm) thickness and a 4-inch (10-cm) diameter. Season generously with salt and pepper.

Preheat a grill to high heat, then clean and oil the grill grates. Alternatively, you can cook these on the stove, preferably in a lightly oiled cast-iron skilled. Grill the burgers until the bottoms are nicely browned, then flip and continue cooking to the desired doneness, 3 to 4 minutes per side for medium (140° to 145°F [60° to 63°C] internal temperature). Thirty seconds before the burgers are done, add the cheese to the patties and cover until they are melted. Let the burgers rest for 5 minutes before assembling. To assemble, slather the green mayo on the bottom buns, then top with lettuce, if using, and the cooked patties. Add desired toppings, and then another dollop of the green mayo and the top buns. Serve immediately!

NOTES
If you don't have a meat grinder at home, ask your butcher to grind the picanha (twice) for you. If grinding at home, make sure your meat is very cold before grinding twice.

PICADINHO NA CERVEJA
(BEEF TIPS IN BEER SAUCE)

There are as many picadinho recipes as there as cooks in Brazil. Every family has a recipe! In my version, succulent and tender beef tips are served in a savory beer gravy that is thickened with a technique I borrowed from French cuisine: the beurre manié. Equal parts butter and flour are used to make a paste, which is then stirred into the sauce to create a rich, irresistible gravy. Serve with Farofa de Banana (Toasted Cassava Flour with Banana; page 77) and rice. You can also top each plate with a fried egg!

FOR THE PICADINHO

1½ lb (680 g) tenderloin, sirloin or equivalent, cut into ¼" (6-mm) chunks

Kosher salt and freshly ground pepper, as desired

½ tsp smoked paprika

1 tbsp (8 g) all-purpose flour

2 tbsp (30 ml) vegetable oil

2 oz (57 g) slab bacon, cut into small cubes

1 small onion, finely chopped

3 cloves garlic, finely minced

1 cup (240 ml) brown ale

½ cup (120 ml) beef stock

1 tsp brown sugar

1 tbsp (15 g) Dijon mustard

1 tbsp (15 g) Worcestershire sauce

1 bay leaf

1 tbsp (4 g) chopped parsley

FOR THE BEURRE MANIÉ

1 tbsp (14 g) butter, softened

1 tbsp (8 g) flour

To make the picadinho: In a large bowl, combine the beef, salt, pepper, paprika and flour. Mix well so all the beef chunks are coated. Heat the vegetable oil in a large skillet over medium-high heat. Add the beef and cook for 2 to 3 minutes, or until browned. Remove to a bowl or plate and reserve. Add the cubed bacon to the skillet and cook for 5 minutes, or until the fat has rendered and the bacon is no longer raw. Stir in the onion and cook for 2 to 3 minutes, or until softened. Add the garlic and cook for 30 seconds to 1 minute, or until fragrant. Pour in the brown ale and cook, using a wooden spoon to loosen all the browned bits from the bottom of the pan, until reduced by half. Add the beef stock, brown sugar, mustard, Worcestershire sauce, bay leaf, and a pinch of salt and pepper. Bring the mixture to a boil, and then lower the heat to medium-low. Return the beef to the pan, cover and simmer for 15 minutes, or until the beef is very tender.

While the beef simmers, make the beurre manié: In a small bowl, stir together the butter and flour. Add the beurre manié to the beef, and cook, uncovered, over medium heat until the gravy thickens. Remove the bay leaf. Taste and adjust the seasoning. Stir in the parsley and serve immediately.

2 large Yukon Gold potatoes, scrubbed clean and thinly sliced

Vegetable oil, for frying

10 cloves garlic, peeled and thinly sliced

Kosher salt and freshly ground pepper, as desired

2 (6–8-oz [170–226-g]) filet medallions (tenderloin)

Farofa, for serving (see Notes)

FILÉ À OSWALDO ARANHA
(FILET MIGNON WITH GARLIC)

This dish, which consists of thick filet medallions topped with deep-fried garlic, is a homage to Oswaldo Aranha, a Brazilian politician and diplomat. Oswaldo was a loyal costumer of Cosmopolita, a restaurant in Rio de Janeiro where he used to ask for this dish for lunch every time he dined there. The entrée was eventually added to the menu and became popular all over the country.

The garlicky medallions are traditionally served with rice, farofa and potato chips (recipe included) that have been fried in the same oil that was used to fry the garlic. It is a great meal to serve as a romantic dinner or whenever you want to impress some guests!

Place the potatoes in a bowl of water. Reserve.

In a saucepan, add 2 inches (5 cm) of oil with the garlic. Cook over medium-high heat for 5 minutes, or until the garlic starts frying and gets golden brown. Remove with a slotted spoon onto a plate lined with paper towels.

While the garlic is frying, drain the potatoes and pat them dry with paper towels. Once the garlic has been removed from the pan, reserve 3 tablespoons (45 ml) of the oil, and then fry the potatoes in the remaining oil, working in batches and placing the cooked potatoes on a wire rack over paper towels to get rid of any excess grease. Season the potatoes generously with salt. Reserve.

Preheat the oven to 400°F (200°C).

Season the medallions generously with salt and pepper. Heat the reserved garlic-infused oil in a large cast-iron skillet or oven-safe skillet, and cook the fillets for 2 minutes per side, or until nicely browned. Transfer the skillet to the oven and continue cooking to the desired doneness (5 minutes for medium). Remove the skillet from the oven and let the fillets rest for at least 5 minutes. Serve the medallions topped with the garlic chips and with the potato chips and farofa on the side.

NOTES
Farofa is a popular Brazilian side dish that consists of toasted manioc/cassava flour (farinha de mandioca) that is cooked with aromatics and various ingredients.

4 ripe plantains

Kosher salt, as desired

½ cup (64 g) cornstarch

½ cup (120 ml) water

Flour, for dusting

3 tbsp (42 g) ghee, divided (see Notes)

1 onion, thinly sliced

2 Roma tomatoes, chopped

3 cloves garlic, finely minced

1 lb (454 g) carne seca, desalted, cooked and shredded (see page 15)

¼ cup (15 g) chopped parsley

NHOQUE DE BANANA DA TERRA COM CARNE SECA
(PLANTAIN GNOCCHI)

Move over, potatoes! Plantains are here to give these pillowy gnocchi a tropical twist and a slight sweetness that pairs really well with salty carne seca. The ripe plantains are roasted until they are super soft and sweet, and then mashed and thickened with cornstarch so they can be rolled into gnocchi. The gnocchi are then quickly panfried in ghee (manteiga de garrafa) until golden brown and topped with carne seca that has been sautéed with aromatics and tomatoes. Absolutely irresistible.

Preheat the oven to 350°F (180°C).

Place the plantains on a baking sheet and roast for 15 minutes, flipping them once halfway through, until their skin has blackened and the flesh is very soft. Let them cool slightly, just so you can handle them, and then peel and mash them in a bowl until smooth. Transfer the mashed plantains to a saucepan, over medium heat and season with a pinch of salt. In a small bowl, dissolve the cornstarch in the water and start adding this mixture gradually, stirring and letting the mashed plantains absorb everything before adding more, to prevent clumps. Cook for 10 minutes, or until the mixture thickens. Let it cool to room temperature, and then refrigerate for 1 hour, or until set.

Dust your counter with flour and divide the mixture into three equal parts. Roll each dough piece into a log shape, then cut into squares. You can use a fork to press down lightly on the side or roll them on a gnocchi board to make a classic gnocchi indentation. Reserve.

Heat 1 tablespoon (14 g) of the ghee in a large skillet over medium heat. Add the onion and cook for 3 to 5 minutes, or until translucent. Stir in the tomatoes and cook for 3 minutes, or until they have softened. Add the garlic and cook for 1 minute, or until fragrant and no longer raw. Stir in the carne seca, mixing well. Let it cook for 5 to 8 minutes, or until it starts to crisp up on the bottom. Taste and season as needed, and then stir in the parsley. Remove to a bowl.

Heat the remaining ghee over medium-high heat. Working in batches, panfry the plantain gnocchi for 2 minutes per side, or until golden and slightly crisp on both sides. Transfer the gnocchi to a serving platter, and then top with the reserved carne seca. Serve immediately!

NOTES
In the North, they use a lot of manteiga de garrafa as their cooking fat. It is very similar to ghee, so here in the U.S., I just use ghee instead.

CHICKEN

FRANGO COM QUIABO
(CHICKEN WITH OKRA)

YIELD: 4 SERVINGS

2 lb (907 g) boneless, skinless chicken thighs

Juice of 1 lime

Kosher salt and freshly ground black pepper, as desired

2 tsp (5 g) sweet paprika

1 lb (454 g) okra (see Notes)

2 tbsp (28 g) unsalted butter

2 tbsp (30 ml) vegetable oil

1 large onion, chopped

1 tomato, cored, seeded and chopped

6 cloves garlic, minced

1 tbsp (16 g) tomato paste

2 cups (480 ml) chicken broth

¼ cup (15 g) chopped parsley

Rice, for serving

NOTES

The sliminess in okra is caused by something called mucilage, which is also present in aloe vera. To get rid of it, and therefore end up with a slime-free okra, it is important to dry the okra really well before cutting and cooking, as water intensifies the effects of the mucilage.

A version of chicken with okra can be found in several different cuisines, including Turkish, Greek, Indian and Creole. This is the Brazilian version, which originates from the state of Minas Gerais and is often served with Angu de Milho (page 70).

What makes our version different are the extra steps we take to make sure the okra isn't slimy. Other cuisines might love okra's viscosity, but Brazilians usually can't stand it. If that's you too, don't worry! Just follow my instructions and you can rest assured that you will be rewarded with a delicious, slime-free meal!

In a large bowl, combine the chicken, lime juice, salt, pepper and paprika. Give it a good massage with your hands so all the chicken thighs are thoroughly coated. Reserve, letting it marinate for 20 minutes while you prepare the other ingredients.

Rinse and dry the okra very well to get rid of any slime. With a sharp knife, remove the edges and cut them into 1-inch (2.5-cm) pieces. Heat the butter in a large braiser or sauté pan over medium-high heat, until melted. Add the okra and cook, stirring constantly for 10 minutes, or until any remaining slime cooks out. Be careful not to overcrowd your pan, otherwise the okra will steam and that will create more slime! Remove from the pan and reserve. Wipe the pan well with paper towels before continuing.

Return the pan to medium-high heat, and add the vegetable oil. Once hot, add the chicken and brown on all sides for 2 to 3 minutes per side. Work in batches if needed so you don't overcrowd the pan. Remove the chicken onto a plate and reserve.

Add more oil to the pan if needed, and then sauté the onion for 3 minutes, or until translucent. Stir in the tomato and cook for 2 minutes, or until softened. Add the garlic and cook for 30 seconds, or until fragrant. Stir in the tomato paste, letting it sauté for 1 to 2 minutes to bring forward its sweetness. Pour in the chicken broth and add a pinch of salt and pepper. Bring to a boil, and then return the chicken to the pan. Lower the heat to a simmer, cover and cook for 20 minutes, or until the chicken is cooked through and a thermometer inserted into the thickest part of the thighs reads at least 165°F (75°C). Add the reserved okra, cover and cook for 2 to 3 minutes. Taste for seasoning and adjust as needed. Stir in the parsley and serve with rice or Angu de Milho (page 70).

2 lb (907 g) chicken breast, cubed

Juice of 1 lime

Kosher salt and freshly ground black pepper, as desired

1 lb (454 g) yuca root, peeled and cut into large chunks (see Notes)

1½ cups (360 ml) chicken broth

1 tbsp (15 ml) olive oil, plus more as needed

1 large onion, chopped

1 red bell pepper, cored, seeded and finely diced

2 Roma tomatoes, chopped

3 cloves garlic, minced

1 small red chile pepper, cored, seeded and chopped

1 tbsp (16 g) tomato paste

1 (13.7-fl oz [403-ml]) can coconut milk

½ cup (120 ml) heavy cream (optional)

1 tbsp (15 ml) dendê (red palm) oil, or to taste (see Notes)

½ cup (8 g) chopped cilantro

Rice, for serving

BOBÓ DE FRANGO
(CHICKEN WITH YUCA STEW)

This recipe is a twist on bobó de camarão, a classic dish from the northeast of Brazil. In this version, we'll use chicken instead of the traditional shrimp, but we'll keep everything else somewhat the same to bring forward those flavors from Bahia that we all cherish and love! Bobó's consistency is usually like a light and creamy porridge, but I prefer it a little thinner. If you like it thicker, just use more yuca than the amount called for in the recipe and omit the heavy cream.

In a large bowl, combine the chicken, lime juice, salt and pepper. Reserve for 15 minutes to marinate.

Place the yuca chunks in a saucepan and cover with water. Cook over medium-high heat for 20 to 30 minutes, or until it starts to boil. Lower the heat to medium-low and continue cooking for 20 to 30 minutes, or until very tender. Drain and transfer to a blender with 1 cup (240 ml) of the hot liquid from the saucepan. Blend until smooth, and then add the chicken broth and blend again to combine. Reserve.

Heat the oil in a large Dutch oven or heavy-bottomed pot over medium-high heat. Add the chicken, working in batches if necessary, and cook for 2 to 3 minutes per side, or until browned. Remove to a plate and reserve. Add more oil if necessary, lower the heat to medium and sauté the onion and bell pepper for 5 minutes, or until the onions are translucent and the bell pepper has softened. Stir in the tomatoes and cook for 2 to 3 minutes, or until the tomatoes soften. Add the garlic and chile pepper, cooking for 1 minute, or until fragrant. Stir in the tomato paste, letting it cook for 1 to 2 minutes, and then stir in the coconut milk. Return the chicken to the pot and cook for 5 minutes, or until the chicken is cooked through. Stir in the reserved yuca mixture, which will thicken the stew considerably. If desired, stir in the heavy cream for extra creaminess. Pour in the dendê oil, and then taste and adjust as needed. Stir in the cilantro and serve immediately with rice!

NOTES
- *Tips on peeling yuca are on page 14.*
- *Dendê oil is a thick, reddish-orange oil extracted from the dendezeiro (palm tree). It is the same as red palm oil, and it can be found at most grocery stores or online. I don't recommend substituting it, as it really imparts a flavor that is characteristic of this dish. That being said, if you can't find it, just omit it.*

FOR THE MARINADE

2 lb (907 g) chicken breast, thinly sliced (see Notes)

1 tbsp (15 ml) low-sodium soy sauce

1 tsp cornstarch

1 tsp sesame oil

FOR THE SAUCE

⅓ cup (80 ml) low-sodium soy sauce

1 cup (240 ml) water

1 tbsp (15 ml) sesame oil

1 tbsp (8 g) cornstarch

FOR THE STIR-FRY

2 tbsp (30 ml) vegetable oil, plus more as needed

2 large onions, cut into petals (see Notes)

1 red bell pepper, cored and diced (see Notes)

1 yellow bell pepper, cored and diced

1 orange bell pepper, cored and diced

2 cloves garlic, finely minced

⅓ cup (49 g) roasted peanuts

Sliced green onions, for garnishing

Rice, for serving

FRANGO XADREZ
(CHICKEN STIR-FRY WITH PEANUTS)

Frango xadrez is the Brazilian version of Sichuan gong bao chicken (or what Americans know as Kung Pao chicken). Our version is not spicy and—unlike the original—calls for onions and bell peppers. This dish is so popular in Brazil that it is now part of most home cooks' repertoire. Served with rice, it makes a delicious and nutritious meal that takes less time to make than it would take to pick up the phone to order takeout!

To make the marinade for the chicken, combine the chicken, soy sauce, cornstarch and sesame oil in a large bowl. Use your hands to thoroughly massage the chicken with the marinade so every piece is coated. Let it sit for at least 15 minutes at room temperature or up to overnight in the fridge.

To make the sauce, whisk together the soy sauce, water, sesame oil and cornstarch in a medium bowl. Reserve.

To make the stir-fry, in a large wok or skillet over medium-high heat, heat the vegetable oil. When shimmering, brown the chicken on all sides for 2 to 3 minutes per side, working in batches if necessary to not overcrowd the pan. Remove the chicken to a plate.

Add more oil if needed. Stir in the onions and the three types of bell peppers and cook for 8 to 10 minutes, or until tender and beginning to brown on the edges. Stir in the garlic and cook for 30 seconds, or until fragrant. Pour in the reserved sauce and cook for 5 minutes, or until thickened. Return the chicken to the pan, cooking just until warm. Stir in the peanuts, garnish with the green onions and serve with rice.

NOTES
The chicken slices, onion petals and diced bell peppers should be roughly the same size.

8 oz (226 g) chicken breast

Kosher salt, as desired

1 tbsp (15 ml) olive oil, divided, plus more for drizzling

1 tbsp (14 g) unsalted butter

1 small onion, finely chopped

3 cloves garlic, finely minced

½ cup (120 ml) tomato passata or tomato sauce

Freshly ground pepper, as desired

1 lb (454 g) pizza dough

⅔ cup (160 ml) pizza sauce

1½ cups (168 g) shredded mozzarella cheese

½ tsp dried oregano

¼ cup (45 g) sliced pitted green olives

1 (8.8-oz [250 g]) pouch catupiry cheese (see Notes)

NOTES

- *If you don't own a pizza stone, place a baking sheet or pizza pan that has been lightly coated in oil in the oven while you assemble your pizza. That will help the bottom cook and crisp up to perfection!*

- *The pizza can also be cooked in an outdoor pizza oven if you own one!*

- *Catupiry is a Brazilian soft, creamy cheese, similar to cream cheese. You can find it at Brazilian stores or online. You can also make it homemade, and I have a recipe for that on the blog!*

PIZZA DE FRANGO COM CATUPIRY

(CREAMY CHICKEN PIZZA)

If I could choose one pizza flavor to represent Brazil, it would be frango com catupiry! You won't find a Brazilian pizzeria that doesn't make it, as this is one of the top five most requested pizzas in the country. Unfortunately, it'll be difficult to find it outside Brazil, so the only solution is to make it at home. Thankfully, it is easy to make and just as delicious as the ones you would order from the pizzerias.

This recipe calls for pizza dough, and I have a great recipe on my blog, but you can also use dough or a premade crust from the grocery store.

Place the chicken breast in an Instant Pot and cover with water. Season generously with salt and cook on high pressure for 10 minutes, letting the pressure release naturally for another 10 minutes. Drain, shred the chicken and reserve.

Heat 1 teaspoon of the oil and the butter in a large skillet over medium heat. Sauté the onion for 2 to 3 minutes, or until translucent. Add the garlic and cook for 1 minute, or until fragrant and no longer raw. Stir in the shredded chicken, mixing well and letting it cook with the other ingredients for 2 to 3 minutes so the flavors meld. Pour in the tomato passata and season with salt and pepper. Lower the heat to low and simmer for 15 to 20 minutes, uncovered. Taste and adjust seasoning as needed. Reserve.

Preheat the oven to as high as it will go (usually around 500°F [260°C]) and place a pizza stone in the bottom third of your oven (see Notes). Stretch the pizza dough to a circle that is 12 to 14 inches (30 to 36 cm) in diameter. You can use a rolling pin if your pizza stretching skills are not pizzaiolo material!

Transfer the dough to a pizza peel, a rimless cookie sheet or upside-down rimmed baking sheet that has been thoroughly dusted with flour. Brush the top of the dough all over with the remaining olive oil. Spread the pizza sauce in an even layer, leaving a ½-inch (1.3-cm) border all around. Top with the mozzarella cheese, followed by the shredded chicken. Sprinkle the oregano and scatter the olives. Season with salt and pepper, and pipe the catupiry cheese, making a large spiral, checkered pattern (like the photo), or just add dollops of creamy cheese all around. Drizzle the pizza with more olive oil, and then transfer to the pizza stone. Bake for 8 to 15 minutes, or until the bottom of the pizza is golden brown and the cheese is nice and bubbly and beginning to brown in some spots. Remove the pizza from the oven and place it onto a cooling rack to cool slightly before slicing and serving!

1 (3–4-lb [1.5–1.8-kg]) whole fryer chicken, spatchcocked

6 cloves garlic, peeled

1 tbsp (14 g) kosher salt, plus more as needed

1 tsp smoked paprika

Freshly ground black pepper, as desired

Juice of 1 lime

¼ cup (60 ml) olive oil

GALETO AO PRIMO CANTO
(OVEN-ROASTED SPATCHCOCKED CHICKEN)

Galeto ao primo canto is a typical chicken dish from the south of Brazil, especially Rio Grande do Sul. It is made with galeto, a young chicken that is harvested at around three weeks old (hence the name "chicken at first song") and usually roasted over coals.

Here in the United States, the closest you will find to a galeto are the young (fryer/broiler) chickens. They are a little older and bigger, but I like them because I can feed four people with just one chicken! If you prefer, you can use Cornish game hens instead, which are similar in age and size as galetos, calculating one Cornish game hen per person.

Spatchcocking your bird will ensure that it cooks quicker and more evenly. If spatchcocking a chicken intimidates you, just ask your butcher to do it for you. They are usually happy to help, and it saves you the trouble and mess from doing it yourself

Preheat the oven to 425°F (220°C).

Pat the chicken dry with paper towels. Loosen up the chicken's skin by sliding your fingers between the meat and the skin at the openings, going as far as you can reach.

With a mortar and pestle, pound and grind the garlic, salt, paprika and black pepper until you achieve a smooth paste. Stir in the lime juice and olive oil. Place half of that mixture inside the chicken skin, using your fingers to spread it all around, and then rub the remaining all over the skin. Season the chicken with salt and pepper.

Place the chicken, breast side up, in a roasting pan or rimmed baking sheet fitted with an oven-safe metal rack. Roast for 45 minutes, or until a thermometer inserted into the thickest part of the thigh reads 165°F (74°C), covering with foil if the chicken is browning too quickly. If desired, you can baste the chicken a couple times with the pan juices. Remove the chicken from the oven, cover it with foil and allow it to rest for 10 minutes before carving and serving.

PORK

LOMBO NA CACHAÇA E MEL
(PORK LOIN WITH CACHAÇA AND HONEY)

YIELD: 4-6 SERVINGS

A roasted pork loin is an easy-yet-delicious way to impress guests at a dinner party or your family for Sunday supper! Imagine the juicy, succulent pork that has been marinated in flavors inspired by a caipirinha (Brazil's national cocktail, with honey, lime and cachaça), and then pan-seared for a beautiful glow before going in the oven where it will roast to perfection. Definitely not your grandma's roast!

The cachaça not only gives the pork loin a Brazilian twist but also provides the acidity that will help tenderize the meat, making the roast very tender with only a hint of cachaça flavor that is not at all overpowering. Make it a meal by serving it with a nice farofa (such as Viradinho de Couve on page 73), rice or a potato side dish, such as roasted, sautéed or mashed potatoes.

YIELD: 4-6 SERVINGS

Juice of 2 limes

1 tbsp (15 ml) honey

⅓ cup (80 ml) cachaça

8 cloves garlic, minced

Kosher salt and freshly ground pink pepper, as desired (see Notes)

2 lb (907 kg) boneless pork loin rib roast, with excess fat trimmed

2 tbsp (30 ml) olive oil

In a medium bowl, whisk together the lime juice, honey, cachaça, garlic, salt and pepper. Place the pork loin roast in a large resealable bag and pour in the marinade, turning a few times so the whole roast is coated. Refrigerate overnight or for up to 48 hours.

Preheat the oven to 375°C (190°C).

Remove the pork roast from the marinade, reserving the marinade for later. Pat it dry with paper towels. Heat the olive oil in a large skillet over medium-high heat, and then brown the pork on all sides for 2 minutes per side. Transfer the roast to a roasting pan, and then pour the marinade over the roast. Roast for 30 to 45 minutes and until a meat thermometer inserted in its thickest part reads at least 145°F (63°C), basting the roast with the pan juices a couple times. Remove the roast from the oven, tent with foil and let it rest for 10 minutes before slicing and serving!

NOTES
Brazilian pink pepper (pimenta rosa) is sweeter, fruitier and milder than black pepper, so use it if you can find it. It adds a beautiful pink dust to whatever you are cooking. Nowadays, you should be able to find it at some local grocery stores or gourmet markets. If not, it is widely available online.

1 tsp olive oil, plus more as needed

4 oz (113 g) slab bacon, finely diced

1 lb (454 g) ground sweet Italian sausage

1 large onion, finely chopped

1 large carrot, peeled and finely diced

1 large celery rib, finely diced

3 cloves garlic, finely minced

Kosher salt and freshly ground black pepper, as desired

½ tsp smoked paprika

1½ cups (234 g) rinsed yellow canjiquinha (corn grits) (see Notes)

7 cups (1.6 L) low-sodium chicken broth, plus more as needed

2 tbsp (28 g) unsalted butter

¼ cup (15 g) chopped parsley

CANJIQUINHA DE LINGUIÇA
(BRAZILIAN GRITS WITH SAUSAGE)

Canjiquinha (corn grits) is one of those cold weather meals that hugs your soul! Also known as péla-égua or quirerada, this is a dish from Minas Gerais that is very popular during our winter festivals (festas juninas). This dish is served as a main dish, sometimes accompanied by sautéed collard greens. The consistency is up to you: Canjiquinha can be thick like American grits or a little looser, like a soup.

In a large Dutch oven or heavy-bottomed pot, heat the olive oil over medium-high heat. Add the bacon and cook for 3 to 5 minutes, or until browned. Remove the bacon with a slotted spoon to a plate and reserve. Add more oil if needed, and add the sausage to the pot, breaking it apart with a wooden spoon and cooking for 5 to 8 minutes, or until crumbled and browned. Remove and reserve with the bacon. Stir in the chopped onion, carrot and celery, and sauté for 5 minutes, or until softened. Add the garlic and sauté for 1 minute, or until fragrant and no longer raw. Return the sausage and bacon to the pot along with the paprika and the canjiquinha, mixing to combine. Season with salt and pepper, and then pour in the chicken broth. Bring to a boil, and then lower to a simmer, cover and cook for 30 to 45 minutes, or until the grits are very soft, giving it a good stir every 10 minutes to prevent it from sticking to the bottom. If necessary, add more broth or water.

Once the canjiquinha is done, you can add up to 2 cups (480 ml) more of broth if it's too thick for your liking. Taste and adjust seasoning, and then stir in the butter and parsley. Serve immediately!

NOTES
Canjiquinha is Brazilian corn grits. It's made from dried and ground corn and is coarser than cornmeal. You can buy the Brazilian brand, Yoki, which sells canjiquinha at Brazilian markets or online, or just grab a bag of corn grits at your local store.

PERNIL AO MOLHO DE ABACAXI
(ROASTED PORK WITH PINEAPPLE SAUCE)

FOR THE PERNIL

1 (5–6-lb [2.3–3-kg]) boneless pork shoulder roast, trimmed of excess fat and tied

1 cup (240 ml) pineapple juice

10–12 cloves garlic

1 onion, peeled and quartered

1 tbsp (14 g) smoked paprika

½ cup (120 ml) olive oil

4 sprigs rosemary, leaves only

Kosher salt and freshly ground black pepper, as desired

1 cup (240 ml) water, plus more as needed (see Notes)

FOR THE SAUCE

½ cup + ⅓ cup (200 ml) water, divided

½ cup (120 ml) pineapple juice

¼ cup (55 g) brown sugar

2 tbsp (30 ml) apple cider vinegar

1 pineapple, cored and cut into small cubes

Kosher salt and freshly ground black pepper, as desired

1 tbsp (8 g) cornstarch

NOTES

Keep an eye on the roast during the roasting time and add more water to the pan as needed. You do not want to let the bottom of the roasting pan dry out and burn because not only can that ruin your pan, but we also need those pan juices to make the sauce!

This is a dish worthy of your holiday table, with tender, slow-cooked pork, served with a pineapple sauce. When I say tender, I mean the roast is so tender and succulent that it falls apart at the mere touch of a fork or knife. Exactly like pernil should be!

In Brazil, pernil is often served for Christmas with a rice pilaf and/or farofa to soak up all the juices. It is such a crowd favorite that you'll be watching everybody dig in while secretly hoping you have leftovers for some next-day pernil sandwiches.

To make the pernil, first check if your roast has the skin on. If so, cut slits in a crisscross pattern into the skin with a small sharp knife and set aside.

Add the pineapple juice, garlic, onion, paprika, olive oil, rosemary, salt and pepper to the jar of a blender. Blend until smooth. Place the roast in a large resealable bag and pour in the marinade. Rub the roast with the marinade, getting into every nook and cranny and making sure all areas of the pork are coated. Place the roast and any excess marinade in a large resealable bag or in a large bowl covered with plastic wrap, and refrigerate overnight or up to 24 hours. The longer you let it marinate, the better the flavors!

Preheat the oven to 300°F (150°C).

Remove the roast from the fridge and let it rest at room temperature for 30 minutes. Place the roast in a roasting pan on a rack and pour the marinade over it. Add the water to the roasting pan. Cover with foil and roast for 2½ hours. Remove the foil, add more water if needed (see Notes), baste with the pan juices and continue roasting, basting a few more times if desired, until golden brown and a kitchen thermometer inserted into its thickest part reads at least 185°F (85°C). If necessary, crank the heat up at the end if the roast is not golden brown. Remove it from the oven to a cutting board to rest for at least 10 minutes.

While the roast rests on the cutting board and the roasting pan is still hot, make the sauce. Pour ½ cup (120 ml) of the water in the pan to deglaze it. Strain the mixture, discarding the solids and reserving the liquid. In a saucepan, combine the strained pan juices, pineapple juice, brown sugar, vinegar, pineapple cubes and salt and pepper. Bring to a boil over medium-high heat, and then lower the heat to medium-low and cook for 10 minutes, or until the pineapple has softened and the sauce has reduced by half. In a bowl, dissolve the cornstarch into the remaining water. Pour this mixture into the sauce and cook for 5 minutes, or until it thickens. Taste and adjust seasoning as needed. Slice the pernil and serve with the sauce.

3 lb (1.5 kg) Yukon Gold potatoes, peeled

Kosher salt, as desired

8 oz (226 g) Calabresa sausage, finely diced (see Notes)

1 small onion, finely chopped

¼ cup (25 g) freshly grated Parmesan cheese

8 oz (226 g) shredded low-moisture mozzarella cheese

7 oz (198 g) catupiry or cream cheese, softened

½ cup (30 g) chopped parsley, divided

Freshly ground pepper, as desired

¼ cup (57 g) unsalted butter

1 cup (240 ml) olive oil, divided

NOTES

Calabresa is the most popular sausage in Brazil, and it's named for its origins in the Calabria region in Italy. It is used in several dishes, like Feijoada na Instant Pot (page 82) and Arroz de Carreteiro (page 88). Made of pork, it is sold precooked and sometimes smoked. Here in New Jersey, I find it easily at my local grocery store. Depending on where you live, you might need to take a trip to the nearest Brazilian store or order it online. If you must substitute, you should choose a precooked, preferably smoked sausage, such as kielbasa, andouille or cured chorizo.

BATATA RECHEADA COM CALABRESA E QUEIJO

(SKILLET POTATO STUFFED WITH CALABRESA AND CHEESE)

Inspired by the Swiss potato rosti—which are very popular in Brazil—this version consists of mashed potatoes enveloping a mixture of cheese and Brazilian Calabresa sausage. It's cooked in a skillet on the stove until crispy on the outside but tender and creamy inside! This quick and delicious meal can be served for lunch or dinner, preferably accompanied by a nice salad!

Place the potatoes in a large saucepan and cover with water. Add a pinch of salt and bring it to a boil over medium-high heat. Once boiling, lower the heat to medium-low and cook for 15 to 20 minutes, or until fork-tender.

While the potatoes are cooking, combine the diced sausage, onion, Parmesan, mozzarella, catupiry and ¼ cup (15 g) of the parsley in a large bowl. Mix well to combine. Season with salt and pepper. Reserve.

When the potatoes are done, drain and let them dry in the colander for a couple of minutes. Transfer to a bowl and mash them until smooth with a fork, potato masher or ricer. Stir in the butter and remaining parsley.

Place a 10½-inch (27-cm) nonstick skillet with sloped sides on the stove over medium-low heat. Pour in ½ cup (120 ml) of the olive oil, swirling the skillet to coat all of the surface. Add half of the mashed potatoes and spread it with a rubber spatula, lightly patting it down to cover the bottom and sides of the skillet. Add the reserved sausage filling, spreading it into a single layer, and then top with the remaining mashed potatoes, gently spreading it to cover the filling and sliding the spatula around the edges to seal it.

Cook the first side over medium-low heat for 15 minutes, or until the bottom is golden and the edges are starting to lift from the pan. Before flipping, run a rubber spatula underneath to ensure nothing is stuck. Cover the skillet with a plate, and then flip it quickly onto the plate. Place the skillet back on the stove and add the remaining olive oil, swirling the skillet to coat it well. Slide the pie back onto the skillet with the golden side up and cook for 15 minutes, or until the second side is also golden and crispy. Slide onto a serving platter and slice in wedges. Serve immediately!

PEIXADA À BAIANA
(FISH STEW IN COCONUT MILK)

YIELD: 4-6 SERVINGS

2 lb (907 g) firm white fish fillets, cut into 2" (5-cm) pieces

1 tsp turmeric

1 tsp hot paprika

1 (4-g) cube fish bouillon, hand crushed

Juice of ½ lime

5 large Yukon Gold potatoes, peeled

Kosher salt, as desired

2 tbsp (30 ml) extra virgin olive oil

1 small red bell pepper, cut into rings

1 small yellow bell pepper, cut into rings

1 small green bell pepper, cut into rings

2 large tomatoes, sliced

1 large onion, sliced

1 (13.7-fl oz [403-ml]) can coconut milk

½ cup (120 ml) water

Freshly ground black pepper, as desired

2 tbsp (4 g) chopped cilantro or parsley

Rice, for serving

In this fish stew, fish fillets simmer with aromatics, bell peppers, tomatoes and potatoes in a flavorful coconut milk broth. It's similar to moqueca baiana, but without the dendê (red palm) oil and with the addition of potatoes, making it a filling meal for a cold evening.

When buying the fish for this dish, choose a boneless white fish that won't fall apart while cooking, such as seabass, dogfish or grouper. In Brazil, fish can be bought already cut in thick chunks (postas), but here in the U.S., you will have to ask the fishmonger to do it for you or buy the fillets and cut them yourself.

In a large bowl, add the fish, turmeric, paprika, crushed bouillon and lime juice. Give it a good toss, using your hands, so all the fish pieces are thoroughly coated. Reserve, letting it marinate for 30 minutes.

Place the potatoes in a large pot and cover with water. Season with salt. Bring them to a boil, lower the heat to medium-low and cook for 8 to 10 minutes, or until they are almost cooked through. (They will continue cooking in the stew.) Drain the potatoes, slice them into 1-inch (2.5-cm)-thick slices and reserve.

Heat the oil in a Dutch oven over medium-low heat. Arrange a layer of potatoes, then bell peppers, tomatoes, onion and fish. Pour half of the coconut milk over the layers, and then arrange a second layer of all the ingredients. Pour in the remaining coconut milk and the water. Season with salt and pepper. Cover, lower the heat to a simmer and cook for 10 to 15 minutes (depending on the thickness of the fillets), or until the fish is cooked through and easily flakes when poked through. Taste and adjust seasoning as needed. Stir in the cilantro and serve with rice!

8 firm, skinless white fish fillets, such as haddock, cod or tilapia

Juice of 1 lime

2 cups (250 g) all-purpose flour

Kosher salt and freshly ground black pepper, as desired

2 eggs

2 cups (480 ml) vegetable oil, for frying

Lime wedges, for serving

PEIXE FRITO
(FRIED FISH FILLETS)

Another of my grandma's famous recipes! Don't let its simplicity fool you, though. There is a reason family members rushed to the table at the sight of her peixe frito! They are crispy, juicy and absolutely irresistible! Grandma always served her fried fish as an entrée, accompanied by rice, sautéed potatoes and salad, but I find that it also makes a great appetizer, served with various dipping sauces.

In a large bowl, add the fish, lime juice, salt and pepper. Combine and let it marinate for 15 minutes. Pat the fish dry with paper towels. In a shallow bowl, combine the flour with a pinch of salt and pepper. Place the eggs in a second bowl, season with salt and lightly whisk them. Set a baking sheet nearby.

Dip the fish fillets in the eggs, letting the excess drip before transferring them to the flour. Coat well in the flour, pressing the flour into the fish with your fingers so it sticks. Place the fish fillets on the baking sheet and reserve.

Heat the oil in a sauté pan or skillet until a kitchen thermometer reads 350°F (180°C). Fry the fish fillets, working in batches if necessary, and flipping so they brown on both sides. It should take 3 minutes per side to cook. Remove the fried fish to a cooling rack set over a plate with paper towels. Serve the fried fish immediately with lime wedges for squeezing.

FOR THE BÉCHAMEL SAUCE

2 tbsp (28 g) unsalted butter

1 onion, finely chopped

2 tbsp (16 g) all-purpose flour

2 cups (480 ml) whole milk, cold or room temperature

1 cup (240 ml) heavy cream

Kosher salt and freshly ground pepper, as desired

FOR THE FISH

2 lb (907 g) firm, skinless white fish fillets

Juice of 1 lime

3 cloves garlic, minced

Kosher salt and freshly ground pepper, as desired

1 cup (125 g) all-purpose flour

3 tbsp (45 ml) olive oil

2 tbsp (28 g) unsalted butter

FOR THE PLANTAINS

1 tsp olive oil

2 tbsp (28 g) unsalted butter

2 large ripe plantains, peeled and cut into diagonal slices ¼" (6-mm) thick (see Notes)

FOR ASSEMBLING AND SERVING

1 cup (112 g) shredded low-moisture mozzarella

½ cup (50 g) freshly grated Parmesan cheese

Rice, for serving

PEIXE À DELÍCIA
(FISH AND PLANTAIN GRATIN)

Brazilian comfort food at its best, peixe à delícia is a traditional dish from Ceará, a state located in the northeastern part of the country. It is essentially a gratin consisting of layers of béchamel sauce, fish (usually freshwater fish), plantains and cheese. The combo of fish with plantains might be unexpected, but I have a feeling you'll fall in love with it, especially when presented in such an indulgent dish!

To make the béchamel sauce, melt the butter in a saucepan over medium-low heat. Add the onion and cook for 3 minutes, or until translucent. Stir in the flour, and stir constantly until a paste forms and changes from white to slightly golden. Gradually add the milk while whisking constantly to prevent lumps. Cook for 3 to 5 minutes, or until the sauce thickens. Stir in the heavy cream and season with salt and pepper. Reserve.

Preheat the oven to 400°F (200°C).

To make the fish, in a bowl, combine the fish with the lime juice, garlic, salt and pepper. Let it marinate for 15 minutes. Pat the fish dry with paper towels and coat the fillets in the flour. Reserve.

In a large skillet over medium-high heat, heat the olive oil and butter. Once the butter has melted, add the fish, working in batches if necessary, and fry for 2 to 3 minutes per side, or until crispy and golden brown, spooning the melted butter over it as it cooks. Remove to a plate and reserve.

To make the plantains, add the oil and butter and cook the plantains for 2 to 3 minutes per side, or until browned on both sides.

To assemble, pour a layer of half of the béchamel sauce on the bottom of a 9 x 13–inch (23 x 33–cm) baking dish. Arrange the fish on top of the sauce, followed by the plantains. Finish with the remaining sauce, the mozzarella and the Parmesan. Bake for 30 to 45 minutes, or until the gratin is bubbly and the cheese has melted and is golden brown in some spots. Remove from the oven and let it cool for 10 minutes before serving with rice.

NOTES

Plantains (bananas-da-terra) are fruits from the banana family. However, even though they look like large bananas, they are starchier, tougher and less sweet than regular bananas, so they aren't usually eaten raw. You will find them at the produce section of your grocery store, sold either green or ripe. The plantains for this dish should be ripe but still firm. If they are too soft, they will fall apart when cooked.

1 lb (454 g) raw shrimp, peeled and deveined (see Notes)

Kosher salt and freshly ground black pepper, as desired

3 tbsp (45 ml) olive oil, divided

5 cloves garlic, minced

Juice of ½ lime

¼ cup (15 g) chopped parsley

Lime wedges, for serving

CAMARÃO À PAULISTA
(SAUTÉED SHRIMP WITH GARLIC)

Camarão à Paulista is a simple yet delicious dish that is a hit at any Brazilian seaside kiosks or bars. It is usually served as an appetizer, but I find that it works just as well as an entrée served on a bed of rice, pasta or couscous, or as a topping for a nice salad.

The secret here is to not overcook the shrimp! Nobody likes rubbery shrimp, so as soon as they turn from translucent to opaque, they're done. If there is still some oil in the pan after frying the shrimp and garlic, make sure to pour it on the shrimp when tossing with the garlic and herbs, as there is a lot of flavor in that oil!

Season the shrimp generously with salt and pepper. Heat 2 tablespoons (30 ml) of the oil in a large skillet over medium-high heat. Fry the shrimp for 2 to 3 minutes per side, or until no longer translucent. Remove to a bowl.

Add the remaining olive oil to the skillet, and then sauté the garlic until golden, being careful not to burn it. Transfer the garlic to the bowl with the shrimp, and then toss with the lime juice, parsley and more salt and pepper, if needed. Arrange the shrimp on a serving platter and serve with lime wedges!

NOTES
For this recipe, tails can be on or off!

2 lb (907 g) raw large shrimp, tails off, peeled and deveined

Kosher salt and freshly ground pepper, as desired

1 tbsp (15 ml) olive oil, plus more as needed

2 tbsp (28 g) unsalted butter

1 large onion, chopped

4 cloves garlic, minced

2 tbsp (16 g) all-purpose flour

1 tbsp (16 g) tomato paste

1 cup (240 ml) whole milk

1 lb (454 g) catupiry cheese or cream cheese

½ tsp freshly ground nutmeg, or to taste

3.5 oz (100 g) shredded mozzarella

White rice, for serving

Shoestring fries (batata palha), for serving

CAMARÃO AO CATUPIRY

(CREAMY SHRIMP)

Camarão ao Catupiry is a Brazilian classic entrée that is always a hit. It is the perfect dish to serve at a dinner party, as nobody can resist this creamy, cheesy and oh, so comforting shrimp dish! It is traditionally made with catupiry cheese, but if you can't find it, I give you permission to substitute it for cream cheese. Nobody will know!

Preheat the oven to 400°F (200°C).

Season the shrimp generously with salt and pepper. Heat the oil in a large skillet over medium-high heat. Sauté the shrimp for 1 to 2 minutes per side, or until cooked through. Remove the shrimp from the skillet to a bowl and reserve.

Lower the heat to medium, and drizzle in some more oil, if needed. Stir in the butter until it's melted. Sauté the onion for 3 minutes, or until translucent. Add the garlic and sauté for 1 minute, or until fragrant. Stir in the flour and cook, stirring constantly for 1 to 2 minutes, or until turning golden and no longer raw. Add the tomato paste and stir to combine, and then start gradually adding the milk, whisking well between additions to avoid lumps. Stir in the catupiry cheese, and then season with salt, pepper and nutmeg. Stir in the shrimp and remove from the stove.

Transfer the creamy shrimp to a baking dish and top with the shredded mozzarella. Bake for 30 to 45 minutes, or until the cheese is melted and golden brown in some spots. Serve with white rice and shoestring fries (batata palha).

VeGETARIANOS

VEGETARIAN DISHES AND SIDES

Sure, most Brazilians are as carnivorous as they come, but our cuisine is also rich in beautiful, seasonal produce. This chapter might not be as robust as the previous chapter, but I think I have chosen recipes that celebrate the veggies Brazil has to offer, such as plantains, collard greens, corn, squash and hearts of palm!

Most of the recipes in this chapter are side dishes, such as Farofa de Banana (Toasted Cassava Flour with Banana; page 77), Viradinho de Couve (Toasted Cassava Flour with Collard Greens; page 73), Quibebe (Mashed Butternut Squash; page 69) and Angu de Milho (Fresh Corn Puree; page 70). But I have also included a few recipes that would work as a vegetarian main dish, such as the Moqueca Vegetariana (Vegetarian Moqueca; page 65), Pamonha de Forno (Corn Casserole; page 66) and Barquinhos de Banana da Terra (Plantain Boats with Cheese; page 74).

Even if you're not vegetarian, I am sure you will love these tasty veggie-forward recipes. They are anything but boring and will bring a taste of Brazil to your table!

2 tbsp (30 ml) olive oil

4 cloves garlic, minced

1 red chile pepper, cored, seeded and finely chopped

2 large red onions, sliced

9 mini sweet red peppers, sliced (see Notes)

3 Roma tomatoes, sliced

1 (14.8-oz [420-g]) can hearts of palm, drained and sliced no less than ¼" (6-mm) thick (see Notes)

1 (15.5-oz [439-g]) can chickpeas, drained

Kosher salt and freshly ground pink pepper, as desired (see Notes)

2 cups (480 ml) unsweetened coconut milk

¼ cup (60 ml) dendê (red palm) oil, or to taste

⅓ cup (5 g) chopped cilantro, or to taste

Rice, for serving

Farofa, for serving (see Notes)

MoQUECA VeGETARIANA
(VEGETARIAN MOQUECA)

This is a vegetarian/vegan version of the classic moqueca baiana, which is traditionally made with fish and/or other seafood. Here we'll use sliced hearts of palm and chickpeas instead for a very flavorful and nutritious veggie main dish that will please even those who don't follow a vegetarian or vegan lifestyle!

I highly recommend you try to find dendê (red palm) oil to make this recipe, as it gives the dish its characteristic flavor and color. If you can't find it at your grocery store, it is easy to find online!

Heat the olive oil in a large Dutch oven or heavy-bottomed pot over medium-low heat. Sauté the garlic and chile pepper for 1 minute, or until fragrant. Arrange half of the onions in the pot in a layer, followed by a layer of half of the sliced peppers, a layer of half of the tomatoes, a layer of half of the hearts of palm and a layer of half of the chickpeas. Season with a pinch of salt and pepper, and then pour in half of the coconut milk. Repeat the process by layering the remaining ingredients, finishing with the remaining coconut milk and the dendê (red palm) oil. Bring to a boil, and then lower the heat to a simmer and cook for 10 to 15 minutes, or until all the vegetables are tender. Turn the heat off and stir in the cilantro. Taste and adjust seasoning as needed. Serve immediately, with rice and farofa.

NoTES

- You can use 3 red bell peppers instead of the mini peppers.

- Hearts of palm (palmitos) are the core of palm plants from South and Central America. They are rarely eaten fresh and usually boiled and processed before they are consumed. You'll most likely find them canned or jarred, whole or pre-sliced, in the canned food aisle of your local grocery store.

- If you can't find pink pepper, black or white pepper can be used instead.

- Farofa is a popular Brazilian side dish that consists of toasted manioc/cassava flour (farinha de mandioca) that is cooked with aromatics and various ingredients.

8 yellow corncobs

½ tsp granulated sugar

⅓ cup (80 ml) whole milk, or as needed

½ tsp kosher salt

3 tbsp (42 g) unsalted butter, softened

½ cup (50 g) freshly grated Parmesan cheese, divided

PAMONHA DE FORNo
(CORN CASSEROLE)

If you're not familiar with pamonha, it is a sweet or savory corn paste that is assembled and boiled in corn husks, similar to Mexican tamales. Popular all over the country, we have whole establishments dedicated just to serving pamonha, usually located roadside to attract those who are driving by.

After many failed attempts at making traditional pamonha in the U.S., I finally admitted defeat. American corn is different than Brazilian, and I couldn't get it to thicken when boiled. The husks are also different, not as wide, so it was difficult to use them as cups for the pamonha mixture without the filling leaking everywhere. The good news is that this is a version that is made in the oven, like a casserole, meaning you won't have to deal with the mess of filling husk cups. It tastes exactly like a savory pamonha, with a very similar texture. It can be served as a side dish, vegetarian main or even as an afternoon snack. If you love pamonha—or corn—this is a must-try!

Preheat the oven to 350°F (180°C).

Stand each ear of corn up in a bowl or plate and, holding it firmly, carefully run a sharp chef's knife down the length of the ear to shave off the kernels. Transfer the kernels to a blender and add the sugar, milk, salt, butter and ¼ cup (25 g) of the Parmesan cheese. Blend until smooth, adding more milk if necessary.

Transfer the batter to a 11 x 7-inch (28 x 18-cm) baking dish that has been coated in butter or nonstick spray. Sprinkle the remaining Parmesan on top, cover in foil and bake for 45 minutes. Remove the foil and continue cooking for 45 minutes to 1 hour, or until golden brown on top and set. Remove the casserole from the oven and let it cool slightly before slicing and serving.

1 (2-lb [907-g]) butternut squash, peeled, seeded and cubed

Pinch of kosher salt, plus more as needed

1 tsp olive oil

5 tbsp (71 g) unsalted butter, divided

1 onion, grated

4 cloves garlic, finely minced

Freshly ground black or white pepper, as desired

⅓ cup (21 g) chopped parsley

QUIBEBE
(MASHED BUTTERNUT SQUASH)

Quibebe is a Brazilian side dish with African and indigenous origins consisting of mashed squash (in this case, butternut) seasoned with aromatics. It is a great accompaniment to chicken, beef, pork or even fish. This recipe can be made with butternut squash (abóbora de pescoço) or kabocha (abóbora Japonesa).

Place the squash in a large pot with a pinch of salt and cover with water. Bring it to a boil over medium-high heat, and cook for 5 to 6 minutes, or until tender. Drain, and then smash with a fork or potato masher. Reserve.

In a Dutch oven or heavy-bottomed pot, heat the olive oil and 2 tablespoons (28 g) of the butter. Once melted, sauté the onion for 3 minutes, or until translucent. Add the garlic and cook for 30 seconds, or until fragrant. Stir in the mashed squash. Season with salt and pepper, and then stir in the remaining butter, mixing vigorously until the butter incorporates and the mixture looks creamy. Stir in the parsley and serve!

8 yellow corncobs

1 cup (240 ml) water

Kosher salt, as desired

½ cup (50 g) shredded Parmesan cheese

2 tbsp (28 g) cold butter

ANGU DE MILHO
(FRESH CORN PUREE)

Angu de milho is the Brazilian version of polenta. Made with fresh corn instead of cornmeal, it is the perfect bed for braised dishes or anything saucy, such as Frango com Quiabo (Chicken with Okra; page 35). When making this recipe, you should use a blender that is powerful enough to extract all the starch from the corn kernels, as we'll discard the solids and use just the corn juice to make the angu (puree). After 20 minutes on the stove, it thickens into a creamy puree that is so irresistible you will want to eat it by the spoonful.

Stand each ear of corn up in a bowl or plate and, holding it firmly, carefully run a sharp chef's knife down the length of the ear to shave off the kernels. Transfer the kernels to a blender and add the water with a pinch of salt. Blend until smooth, and then strain into a Dutch oven or heavy-bottomed pot, discarding the solids.

Cook over medium-low heat for 20 minutes, or until thickened to a soft polenta consistency. Stir in the Parmesan cheese, taste and adjust salt as needed. Remove from the heat, and then stir the butter, stirring vigorously to combine. Serve immediately.

1½ lb (680 g) rinsed collard greens

3 tbsp (45 ml) olive oil

1 onion, chopped

4 cloves garlic, minced

½ tsp crushed red pepper flakes (optional)

Kosher salt and freshly ground black pepper, as desired

3 cups (420 g) toasted manioc/cassava flour

¼ cup (15 g) chopped parsley

VIRADINHO DE COUVE
(TOASTED CASSAVA FLOUR WITH COLLARD GREENS)

This is a type of farofa dish cooked with collard greens. If you're not familiar with farofa, it is a popular Brazilian side that consists of toasted manioc/cassava flour (farinha de mandioca) that is cooked with aromatics and various ingredients. It is a very versatile side dish, pairing great with anything from rice and beans to a nice roasted pork. I have kept this recipe vegan, but you can also add bacon and/or eggs if you desire.

Remove the stems from the collard greens, stack the leaves and then roll them tightly into a cigar-shaped cylinder. Cut into thin ribbons, and then roughly chop them. Reserve.

In a large skillet, heat the olive oil over medium heat. Add the onion and sauté for 3 minutes, or until translucent. Stir in the garlic and red pepper flakes (if using) and cook for 30 seconds, or until fragrant. Slowly stir in the collard greens, mixing to combine. Season with salt and pepper to taste. Cook for 5 to 8 minutes, or until the collard greens are wilted. Stir in the toasted cassava flour, and cook for 2 to 3 minutes, or until the cassava flour is warm. Stir in the parsley. Taste, adjust seasoning as needed and serve!

NOTES

- *Farinha de mandioca (Brazilian manioc/cassava flour) is the flour that results from soaking and grinding the cassava root, and then drying the pulp to produce a coarse meal. It is sold toasted (torrada) or white (untoasted), and used in a plethora of Brazilian dishes, from farofa to Virado à Paulista (Pork Chops with Rice and Refried Beans; page 85) and Bolinhos de Feijoada (Feijoada Croquettes; page 100). Don't confuse this with the manioc/cassava starch that is sold at the grocery store here in the U.S., as that is powdered starch that is used for other purposes, such as gluten-free baking.*

- *In short, you won't find the type of manioc/cassava flour that we need for Brazilian dishes at a regular grocery store in the U.S., you will need to either make a trip to a Brazilian grocery store or buy it online.*

4 plantains, peeled

1 tbsp (15 ml) melted unsalted butter

4 oz (113 g) shredded mozzarella cheese

Cinnamon sugar (optional)

BARQUINHOS DE BANANA DA TERRA
(PLANTAIN BOATS WITH CHEESE)

These cheese-stuffed plantains are my current favorite snack! I've eaten this for lunch more times than I can count. Sweet, tender plantains filled with ooey-gooey cheese—what's not to love? In Brazil, these are usually served as an afternoon snack, dusted with cinnamon sugar. However, I find that they also make a great side dish or even vegetarian main, similar to the Cuban plátanos maduros, pairing great with rice and beans. If you're in the mood for something heartier, these also pair well with pork.

Preheat the oven to 400°F (200°C).

Place the plantains in a baking sheet and brush them generously with the butter. Bake for 15 minutes, and then, using tongs, flip them and bake for another 15 minutes, or until browned on both sides.

With a paring knife, cut a long slit in the center of each plantain, forming the "boats." Be careful not to cut all the way through the bottoms, or the cheese will leak. Fill each plantain with the mozzarella. Return the boats to the oven and bake for 10 minutes, or until the cheese has melted. If desired, sprinkle with cinnamon sugar before serving!

1 tbsp (15 ml) olive oil

3 tbsp (42 g) unsalted butter

1 small red onion, thinly sliced

2 cloves garlic, minced

2 large bananas, sliced into ½"
(1.3-cm)-thick pieces (see Notes)

2 cups (280 g) toasted manioc/
cassava flour (See Notes)

Kosher salt and freshly ground black
pepper, as desired

Fresh parsley (optional)

FAROFA DE BANANA
(TOASTED CASSAVA FLOUR WITH BANANA)

Another farofa recipe, this time featuring bananas! Because if there's one thing Brazilians love to eat with rice and beans, it's bananas. It especially pairs great with Picadinho na Cerveja (Beef Tips in Beer Sauce; page 28).

The secret here is to not overcook the bananas. We want them to retain their shape and texture instead of cooking down to a mush. Likewise, when stirring in the manioc/cassava flour (farinha de mandioca), be gentle so you don't break down the bananas too much.

Heat the olive oil and butter in a large skillet over medium heat, until the butter has melted, turns an amber color and starts smelling nutty. Be careful not to burn it! Add the onion and sauté for 3 minutes, until softened. Stir in the garlic and cook for 30 seconds, or until fragrant. Add the bananas and sauté for 1 to 2 minutes. You don't want to cook them for too long or they will get too soft and fall apart. Slowly stir in the toasted cassava flour, gently stirring to combine. Cook for 3 to 5 minutes, or until the flour gets slightly crunchy, and then season with salt and pepper. Serve immediately, garnished with chopped fresh parsley, if desired.

NOTES
- *When buying the bananas, choose ones that are not so ripe. They shouldn't be green, but overripe bananas will be too soft to use for this dish!*
- *Manioc/cassava flour can be found online. If you can't find it, corn flour (or even breadcrumbs) can be used instead!*

ARROZ E FEIJÃO

RICE AND BEAN DISHES

Rice and beans are the heart and soul of Brazilian cuisine! Not a single day goes by without one (or both) of them making an appearance at lunch or dinner tables all over Brazil. We even have a never-ending national quarrel: Should the beans be served alongside or on top of the rice? As long as you don't answer "under the rice", you will definitely find people on your side, as we are pretty much divided as a nation on this matter!

In this chapter, you will find Brazil's national dish, Feijoada na Instant Pot (Instant Pot Black Bean Stew; page 82) as well as other entrées and sides such as Baião de Dois (Brazilian Rice with Black-Eyed Peas, Beef and Cheese; page 81) and Virado à Paulista (Pork Chops with Rice and Refried Beans; page 85)—all featuring these beloved ingredients.

FOR THE RICE

1 cup (200 g) long-grain white rice, rinsed

1 tbsp (14 g) clarified butter or ghee

1 medium yellow onion, finely chopped

4 cloves garlic, minced

1 tsp kosher salt

¼ tsp ground turmeric

1¾ cups (420 ml) hot water

1 bay leaf

FOR THE BAIÃO DE DOIS

3 tbsp (42 g) clarified butter or ghee, divided

4 oz (113 g) slab bacon, diced

1 large red onion, finely chopped

4 cloves garlic, minced

1 cup (85 g) shredded carne seca or corned beef (see Notes)

1 (14-oz [397-g]) can black-eyed peas, drained

Kosher salt and freshly ground pepper, as desired

½ cup (120 ml) low-sodium beef broth

5 oz (142 g) grilling cheese such as queijo coalho or halloumi, sliced ¼" (6 mm) thick

⅓ cup (21 g) chopped parsley or cilantro

BAIÃO DE DOIS

(BRAZILIAN RICE WITH BLACK-EYED PEAS, BEEF AND CHEESE)

This is a hearty dish from the northeast of Brazil, consisting of rice, black-eyed peas (or feijão de corda), bacon, carne seca and cheese. It is a meal in itself, and while no accompaniments are necessary, it goes great with a side green salad, vinaigrette (Brazilian salsa) and fried yuca.

The curious name comes from a typical folk dance called baião, which is danced in an intimate, close embrace. Here, the "two" (dois) are the rice and beans, coming together in a delicious baião that will have you begging for more!

To make the rice, place the rice in a fine-mesh strainer and rinse under cold running water until the water runs clear. Reserve. Heat the clarified butter in a saucepan over medium heat. Once hot, add the onion and sauté for 2 to 3 minutes, or until softened. Add the garlic and sauté for 1 minute, or until fragrant. Add the rice and sauté for 1 to 2 minutes, or until it starts clumping together. Stir in the salt and turmeric, and then pour in the hot water. Give it a good mix, add the bay leaf and bring to a boil. Cover, lower the heat and simmer for 15 minutes. Turn the heat off and crack the lid open slightly. Let it rest for 20 minutes, remove the bay leaf and then fluff the rice with a fork. Reserve.

To make the baião de dois, in a large sauté pan, over medium heat, add 2 tablespoons (28 g) of the clarified butter. Once melted, add the bacon and cook for 2 to 3 minutes, or until beginning to turn golden. Stir in the red onion and sauté for 3 minutes, or until softened. Add the garlic and sauté for 1 minute so it releases its aroma. Add the carne seca, stirring to combine. Let it cook for 3 to 5 minutes, or until it begins to crisp up. Stir in the black-eyed peas, the cooked rice and a pinch of salt and pepper. Give it a good stir, and then pour in the beef broth. Cover, lower the heat to medium-low and cook for 5 minutes.

Heat the remaining clarified butter in a nonstick skillet over medium heat. Add the sliced cheese in a single layer and allow it to cook for 2 minutes, without disturbing. Once the bottoms are golden brown, flip and cook the other side for 1 to 2 minutes, or until the slices get nicely golden. Remove to a cutting board and cut into cubes, reserving a few to use as a garnish. Stir the remaining into the baião de dois, along with the parsley. Taste and adjust seasoning as needed. Garnish with the reserved cheese and serve immediately.

NOTES

This dish is traditionally made with carne seca, but cooked corned beef can be used instead. If using corned beef, I recommend not only shredding but also chopping it so the strands are not too long. If using carne seca, you should desalt and cook it according to directions on page 15.

1.1 lb (500 g) carne seca, desalted (see page 15 for desalting instructions)

3 cups (582 g) dry black beans (see Notes)

8 oz (226 g) smoked pork loin (see Notes)

8 oz (226 g) paio sausage (see Notes)

1 tbsp (15 ml) vegetable oil, plus more as needed

8 oz (226 g) Calabresa sausage, sliced (see Notes)

4 oz (113 g) slab bacon, cut into small cubes

1 large onion, chopped

6 cloves garlic, minced

3 bay leaves

FEIJOADA NA INSTANT POT
(INSTANT POT BLACK BEAN STEW)

I couldn't publish a Brazilian cookbook without including a recipe for feijoada. It is our national dish, after all! Feijoada is black beans cooked with smoked meats, creating a rich and hearty stew that is simply to die for. This version is cooked completely in the Instant Pot, which means it can be on the table in an hour. That being said, this is a dish that really benefits from some time in the fridge, tasting even better when reheated the next day! It is worth mentioning that this recipe is easy to adapt, so you can use whatever you have on hand. It can even be made vegetarian or vegan!

Make sure the cuts of pork (or beef) you choose to use for this recipe are not too delicate, or they can fall apart while cooking

The night before you plan on making feijoada, desalt the carne seca (page 15). Place the beans in a large bowl and cover with water. Let them soak overnight in the fridge (see Notes).

The day of, cut the pork loin and paio sausages into 1½- to 2-inch (4- to 5-cm) pieces. Turn your Instant Pot on sauté mode, and once it indicates it's hot, add the oil. Working in batches, brown the smoked pork loin, paio sausage, carne seca and Calabresa sausage. You can add a little more oil between batches, if necessary. Transfer the browned pieces to a bowl and reserve.

Once all the big pieces are browned, add the bacon, and cook for 3 to 5 minutes, or until golden brown. Stir in the onion and cook for 2 to 3 minutes, or until translucent. Use the moisture from the onion to deglaze the Instant Pot, lifting all the browned bits from the bottom. Add the garlic and cook for 1 minute, or until fragrant and no longer raw. Drain the soaked beans and add them to the Instant Pot along with the reserved meat and the bay leaves. Pour in enough water to cover everything, making sure it doesn't go past the max line. Cover and seal the Instant Pot, setting it to cook at high pressure for 30 minutes, with 10 minutes of natural release.

(continued)

Kosher salt and freshly ground black pepper, as desired

Rice, for serving

Farofa, for serving

Collard greens, for serving

Bananas Milanese, for serving (page 87)

Orange slices, for serving

FEIJOADA NA INSTANT POT
(CONTINUED)

Remove the lid and check the beans and meat for doneness. If necessary, cook for 5 to 10 minutes longer, or until the beans are tender and the meat is done. Set the Instant Pot to sauté mode. Remove 2 tablespoons (22 g) of the beans (without liquid) to a small plate, and then mash them with a fork to form a paste. Return this paste to the Instant Pot and boil the stew until it thickens slightly. Remove and discard the bay leaves, and then taste and season the stew with salt and pepper as needed. Serve immediately, with rice, farofa, collard greens, bananas Milanese and orange slices.

NOTES

- *Soaking the beans overnight will make them cook faster. If you forgot, it's okay. You can still make this recipe; they just might take a bit longer to cook!*

- *Depending on where you live, some of the pork cuts and/or sausages called for in this recipe may be hard to find. You can substitute the carne seca for corned beef (without the seasoning pack) and the sausages for any smoked sausages available near you, such as chorizo or kielbasa.*

FOR THE TUTU DE FEIJÃO

1 tsp olive oil

3 oz (85 g) slab bacon, finely diced

1 onion, finely chopped

3 cloves garlic, finely minced

1½ cups (307 g) dry pinto beans, preferably soaked overnight

4½ cups (1 L) cold water

2 bay leaves

½–1 cup (70–140 g) manioc/cassava flour

Kosher salt and freshly ground black pepper, as desired

FOR THE RICE

1 tbsp (15 ml) vegetable oil

1 onion, finely chopped

3 cloves garlic, finely minced

2 cups (400 g) long grain white rice, rinsed

Kosher salt, as desired

3½ cups (840 ml) hot water

FOR THE COLLARD GREENS

1 large bunch fresh collard greens

3 tbsp (45 ml) olive oil

4 cloves garlic, minced

Kosher salt, as desired

VIRADO À PAULISTA
(PORK CHOPS WITH RICE AND REFRIED BEANS)

Virado à Paulista is a whole-meal dish from the state of São Paulo. The dish varies according to the establishment (or cook) that is serving it, but usually consists of pork chops, sausage, rice, a chunky bean puree, collard greens, fried bananas and a fried egg.

Legend has it that Dom Pedro I ate this dish on his way from Rio de Janeiro to São Paulo, where he performed the "Grito do Ipiranga" ("Cry of Ipiranga"), proclaiming Brazil's independence from Portugal. I don't know if that's true, but I can definitely see how a generous meal like that would tide him over for such a long journey!

To make the tutu de feijão, set an Instant Pot to sauté mode and heat the olive oil. Add the bacon and cook for 3 to 5 minutes, or until golden. Stir in the onion and cook for 2 to 3 minutes, or until translucent. Add the garlic and cook for 30 seconds, or until fragrant and no longer raw. Stir in the beans, water and bay leaves. Cook at high pressure for 20 minutes with a 10-minute natural release. Discard the bay leaves. Remove half of the beans and liquid to a blender and blend until smooth. Return the blended beans to the pot, then set the Instant Pot to sauté mode. Gradually add the manioc/cassava flour to achieve the desired consistency. I like mine thinner, so I add ½ cup (70 g) of the flour. If you like it thicker, you might need closer to 1 cup (140 g). Don't worry if you overdo it! You can fix it by adding water. Add salt and pepper to taste. Reserve while you make the rice.

To make the rice, in a large saucepan or small Dutch oven, heat the vegetable oil over medium heat. Once hot, add the onion and sauté for 2 to 3 minutes, or until translucent. Add the garlic and sauté for 30 seconds, or until fragrant and no longer raw. Stir in the rice and sauté for 1 to 2 minutes. Season generously with salt, and then pour in the hot water. Bring it to a boil, then cover and lower the heat to a simmer. Cook for 20 minutes, and then turn the heat off, crack the lid open and let it rest untouched for 15 minutes. Fluff with a fork and reserve.

To make the collard greens, rinse and dry the collard greens, and then remove the center steam of each leaf, stack the leaves together and roll them tightly into a cigar-shaped cylinder. Using a sharp chef's knife, cut them into very thin ribbons and reserve.

Heat the olive oil in a large skillet over medium heat. Add the garlic and cook for 1 minute, or until fragrant. Stir in the collard greens and sauté, tossing so they get thoroughly coated in the garlicky oil. Cover the skillet and cook for 5 minutes, or until the collard greens are wilted and crisp-tender. Season with salt to taste and reserve.

(continued)

FOR THE BANANAS MILANESE

¾ cup (94 g) all-purpose flour

2 eggs, beaten

¾ cup (81 g) plain breadcrumbs

1 tsp kosher salt

2 bananas, peeled and cut into 2" (5-cm) pieces

Vegetable oil, for frying

FOR THE MEAT

4 boneless pork chops

Kosher salt and freshly ground pepper, as desired

1 tbsp (15 ml) vegetable oil

4 Calabresa sausages (see Notes)

Fried eggs, for serving

VIRADO À PAULISTA
(CONTINUED)

To make the bananas Milanese, place the flour in one bowl, the eggs in another and the breadcrumbs in a third. Season the breadcrumbs with the salt. Dip each banana piece in the flour, then dunk in the egg before coating with breadcrumbs.

Heat a small pot with 3 inches (8 cm) of oil over medium-high heat. When the oil reaches 350°F (180°C), start frying the breaded bananas, working in batches so you don't overcrowd the pot. Remove the bananas Milanese to a plate lined with paper towels. Reserve.

To prepare the meat, season the pork chops generously with salt and pepper. Reserve.

Heat the oil in a large skillet over medium-high heat. Add the sausages and fry for 3 to 4 minutes, and then flip and cook for 3 to 4 minutes, or until golden brown and heated through. Remove to a plate and reserve.

Add the pork chops to the skillet, working in batches if necessary, and cook for 5 minutes per side, or until browned on both sides and a meat thermometer registers 140 to 145°F (60 to 63°C). Remove the pork chops to the plate with the sausages and let them rest for at least 5 minutes before serving. Assemble the plates with a little bit of everything, and then serve with fried eggs!

NOTES
If you can't find Calabresa sausage, you can use any fully cooked sausage, such as kielbasa, preferably smoked.

1 tbsp (15 ml) vegetable oil, plus more as needed

3 oz (85 g) slab bacon, finely diced

5 oz (142 g) Calabresa sausage, finely diced

1 onion, finely chopped

3 cloves garlic, finely minced

8 oz (226 g) carne seca, desalted, cooked and shredded (page 15)

⅓ cup (80 ml) chicken broth

4 cups (744 g) cooked white rice

Kosher salt and freshly ground black pepper, as desired

⅓ cup (21 g) chopped parsley

ARROZ DE CARRETEIRO
(RICE WITH BACON, SAUSAGE AND DRIED BEEF)

Also known as simply carreteiro or Maria-Isabel, this dish consists of rice mixed with meats such as bacon, sausage and carne seca (dried beef). This dish's name translates in English as wagoner's rice. It gets the name because it was a dish that was easy for wagoners to prepare on the go, since they could take smoked/dried meats with them without the need of refrigeration.

This recipe can be doubled or tripled to feed a crowd, and you can substitute the sausage and meat used, making use of whatever you have on hand! In the south of Brazil, gaúchos will often use leftover grilled beef from a barbecue instead of carne seca.

In a large sauté pan or skillet, heat the oil over medium-high heat. Add the bacon and cook for 3 to 5 minutes, or until golden brown. Remove the bacon with a slotted spoon to a bowl. Add more oil if needed, and then brown the sausage for 2 to 3 minutes per side. Stir in the onion and cook for 2 to 3 minutes, or until translucent. Add the garlic and cook for 30 seconds, or until fragrant and no longer raw. Add the carne seca and cook for 3 to 5 minutes, or until it begins to crisp up in parts. Return the bacon to the pan, and then add the broth. Deglaze the pan with a wooden spoon to scrape off all the browned bits from the bottom. Cook for 5 minutes, or until it is reduced by half. Stir in the rice, and then season with salt and pepper. Cook for 3 to 5 minutes to warm up the rice. Stir in the parsley and serve!

2 lb (907 g) beef oxtail

Kosher salt and freshly ground black pepper, as desired

1 tbsp (15 ml) vegetable oil

2 onions, finely chopped

3 Roma tomatoes, finely chopped

4 cloves garlic, minced

½ cup (120 ml) dry red wine

1 tbsp (15 ml) Worcestershire sauce

3 cups (720 ml) low-sodium beef broth, plus more as needed

2 bay leaves

2 cups (400 g) uncooked long grain white rice, rinsed

⅓ cup (21 g) chopped parsley

ARROZ DE RABADA
(OXTAIL RICE)

This is a hearty and rich dish that consists of slowly braised oxtail that is so tender it falls off the bone and rice that cooks right in the resulting broth from braising the meat. That means that every single bite is bursting with flavor! Definitely a special-occasion, indulgent dish for when you want to impress some friends.

When choosing the oxtails for this recipe, choose large ones with plenty of meat on them, with some fat but not too much. We'll braise the oxtails whole, but will use just the shredded meat in the final dish.

Pat dry the oxtail pieces with a paper towel, and then season them generously with salt and pepper. In a large Dutch oven or heavy-bottomed pot, heat the oil over medium-high heat. Add the oxtails and sear for 3 to 4 minutes per side, or until golden brown on all sides. Remove to a plate and reserve.

Reduce the heat to medium. Add the onions and cook for 2 to 3 minutes, or until translucent. Add the tomatoes and cook for 5 minutes, or until they've softened. Stir in the garlic and cook for 1 minute, or until fragrant. Pour in the wine and deglaze the pot with a wooden spoon to release all the browned bits from the bottom of the pot. Cook for 3 to 5 minutes, or until reduced by half. Stir in the Worcestershire sauce and beef broth. Season with salt and pepper. Bring to a boil, and then add the bay leaves and return the oxtail pieces to the pot. Reduce the heat to low and simmer for 2 to 3 hours, turning the oxtails every now and then, or until the meat is very tender. Remove the oxtails and shred the meat, discarding any big fatty pieces and the bone/cartilage. Reserve.

Skim off any fat that has risen to the surface of the sauce in the Dutch oven. Stir in the rice, cover and cook, stirring every now and then to prevent the rice from sticking to the bottom of the pot, for 15 to 20 minutes, or until the rice is tender. You can stir in some more broth if desired, for a looser consistency. Taste and adjust seasoning as needed. Stir in the shredded oxtail and the parsley and serve!

1 lb (454 g) salted cod (see Notes)

¼ cup (60 ml) extra virgin olive oil

1 yellow onion, chopped

1 red bell pepper, seeded, cored and chopped

1 yellow bell pepper, seeded, cored and chopped

1 orange bell pepper, seeded, cored and chopped

1 large tomato, seeded and chopped

3 cloves garlic, minced

2 tsp (5 g) sweet paprika

½ tbsp (8 g) tomato paste

6 cups (1 kg) cooked white rice

½ cup (90 g) sliced pitted kalamata olives

1 cup (60 g) chopped parsley

Kosher salt, as desired

ARROZ DE BACALHAU

(SALTED COD RICE)

Most cod dishes that you'll find in Brazil—like this one—are actually Portuguese recipes or adaptations of those recipes. However, they have become such a strong part of Brazilian cuisine that it'd be impossible to talk about Brazilian food without talking about them!

Thankfully, it is easy to find salted cod here in the U.S., so anyone can make this recipe at home. Just make sure you go through the steps to desalt the cod and that you taste the dish before adding any salt, as you don't want to end up with a dish that is too salty and impossible to fix!

In Brazil, this dish makes its appearance on Good Friday (Sexta-Feira Santa), when most Brazilians will abstain from eating meat and will eat fish instead.

To desalt the codfish, remove and discard the cod's skin. If the cod pieces are large, cut them into smaller chunks so they can fit in a bowl. Place the pieces in a bowl and cover with cold water. Place in the fridge for 24 to 48 hours, draining and changing the water every 4 hours.

Bring a large pot of water to a boil, and then add the cod pieces. Cook for 2 to 3 minutes, and then drain. Once the cod is cool enough to handle, use your hands to shred into smaller pieces. Reserve.

In a large Dutch oven or heavy-bottomed pot, heat the olive oil over medium heat. Add the onion and sauté for 2 to 3 minutes, or until translucent. Add the bell peppers and tomato, and cook for 3 to 4 minutes, or until softened. Stir in the garlic and sauté for 1 minute, or until fragrant. Stir in the shredded cod, sweet paprika and tomato paste, mixing to combine. Add the cooked rice and olives. Cook for 3 to 5 minutes, or until the rice is heated through. Stir in the parsley, and taste and adjust salt as needed. Serve immediately.

NOTES

Dried and salted cod is codfish that has been dried and salted for preservation. It is very popular in Brazil and used to make the recipes that we've inherited (or adapted) from the Portuguese, such as this dish and Pastel de Bacalhau (page 112). It can be easily found at the fish section of your grocery store. The few times I have not found it myself, I've had luck just asking the fishmonger for it.

2 cups (368 g) dry pinto beans, preferably soaked overnight

1 tbsp (15 ml) olive oil

1 onion, finely chopped

1 large leek, white and light green parts only, thinly sliced

1 celery rib, finely diced

1 carrot, peeled and finely diced

3 cloves garlic, finely minced

2.5 qt (2.5 L) water, divided, plus more as needed

3 bay leaves

Kosher salt and freshly ground black pepper, as desired

1 cup (112 g) ditalini or small-shell pasta

⅓ cup (21 g) chopped parsley

Freshly grated Parmesan cheese, for serving

SOPA DE FEIJÃO COM MACARRÃO
(BEAN AND PASTA SOUP)

Cold weather calls for a soul-warming soup! This is the Brazilian version of the Italian pasta e fagioli, with the main difference being the fact that we blend the beans down to a creamy broth.

The pasta is cooked right in the soup, releasing its starch and making the soup even creamier. That being said, this soup isn't supposed to be thick, more brothy instead, so make sure to adjust the amount of water once the pasta is done cooking. You will also need to add water if the soup cools down and you wish to reheat it, as this soups thickens considerably when it cools. And, while I've kept this recipe vegetarian, you can definitely top this soup with crumbled bacon or sausage. Whatever you do, don't forget the freshly grated Parmesan for serving!

If you can, soak the beans overnight. Just place them in a bowl, cover with water and refrigerate until the next day. Then drain and use as directed. Soaking the beans will help them cook faster.

In a large Dutch oven or heavy-bottomed pot over medium heat, add the olive oil, and when hot, add the onion, leek, celery and carrot and sauté for 5 minutes, or until softened. Add the garlic and sauté for 1 minute, or until fragrant and no longer raw. Stir in the beans, and then pour in 6 cups (1.4 L) of the water and add the bay leaves. Bring it to a boil, and then lower the heat to a simmer, cover and cook until the beans are tender. Depending on how old your beans are and if they've been soaked, this can take anywhere from 1 to 3 hours. If you wish to speed this up, you can cook them in the Instant Pot for 25 minutes on high pressure.

Once the beans are cooked, remove and discard the bay leaves, and then season generously with salt and pepper. Transfer to a blender, or use an immersion blender, adding more water if needed, and blend until smooth, adding more water if needed. Return the blended mixture to the pot over medium heat, and add the remaining water. Taste and adjust seasoning. Stir in the pasta, and simmer for 15 to 20 minutes, or until the pasta is tender. Add more water if necessary to achieve your desired consistency. Stir in the parsley and serve topped with Parmesan!

PETISCOS

SNACKS, APPETIZERS AND BAR FOOD

We Brazilians love our petiscos! I simply couldn't write a book on Brazilian cooking without featuring them. I'd probably be exiled!

Either on weekends or at happy hour, chances are you can find us at the nearest boteco (a hole-in-the-wall bar) sharing food and ice-cold beers with friends. This chapter features some of my favorites, from fried finger foods like the Bolinhos de Feijoada (Feijoada Croquettes; page 100) and baked pastries to a few stuffed breads such as Pão de Calabresa (Sausage Bread; page 116). These are all easy to make at home and perfect for when you need to entertain a crowd! And while they are meant for sharing, no one will judge you if you want to make them to enjoy by yourself. Been there, done that!

So what do you say? Ready to crack open a cold one and share some delicious snacks with me?

FOR THE CRUST

2 cups (480 g) all-purpose flour

1 tsp kosher salt

¾ cup (170 g) unsalted butter, softened

1 large egg

1 egg yolk

Cold water (optional)

Egg wash for brushing the empadinhas

FOR THE FILLING

1 lb (454 g) chicken breast

Kosher salt, as desired

1 tbsp (15 ml) olive oil

1 tbsp (14 g) butter

1 small onion, finely chopped

1 Roma tomato, finely diced

3 cloves garlic, finely minced

½ cup (90 g) chopped pitted green olives

Hot sauce, as desired

⅓ cup (80 ml) tomato sauce

½ cup (120 ml) chicken broth

⅓ cup (80 ml) whole milk

1 tbsp (8 g) flour

Freshly ground black pepper, as desired

4 oz (113 g) catupiry cheese or cream cheese

¼ cup (15 g) chopped parsley

NOTES

If you don't own egg tart molds, you can use a cupcake pan instead. Sizes and number of empadinhas will vary.

EMPADINHAS DE FRANGO
(MINI CHICKEN PIES)

Empadinhas are small hand pies with origins in the Portuguese pastelões, which were large, savory pies. They are often served as appetizers, snacks or finger food at parties. The melt-in-your-mouth buttery pastry envelops a creamy, savory chicken filling that is jeweled with plump olives for bursts of flavor in every bite. You can serve your empadinhas while they are still warm or at room temperature. They can also be reheated, so it's okay to make them ahead and refrigerate until you are ready to serve them!

To make the crust, in a large bowl, combine the flour and salt. Add the butter and, using your fingertips or a pastry cutter, work it into the flour until the mixture resembles coarse sand. Add the egg and egg yolk and mix just until a smooth dough comes together. If necessary, transfer to the counter and knead gently so it's smooth. You shouldn't need any water, but if absolutely necessary, you can add a little bit of cold water, 1 teaspoon at a time. Wrap the dough in plastic and refrigerate for 40 minutes.

To make the filling, place the chicken breast in an Instant Pot and cover with water. Season with a pinch of salt. Cook on high pressure for 15 minutes, with a 10-minute natural release. Drain, shred and reserve.

Turn your Instant Pot to sauté mode. Once hot, heat the oil and butter until the butter has melted. Sauté the onion for 3 minutes, or until translucent. Add the tomato and cook for 3 to 5 minutes, or until softened. Stir in the garlic and cook for 30 seconds, or until fragrant and no longer raw. Add the shredded chicken and cook 2 to 3 minutes, or until the flavors meld. Stir in the olives, hot sauce (a couple of dashes should do), if using, tomato sauce and chicken broth. Cook for 5 to 8 minutes, or until the liquid is almost all evaporated. In a bowl, whisk together the milk and flour. Pour the mixture into the Instant Pot and cook for 5 minutes, or until it thickens. Season with salt and pepper, and then stir in the catupiry and parsley. Remove from the pot and reserve so it cools to room temperature.

Preheat the oven to 350°F (180°C).

Grab a 2-tablespoon (30-g) portion of dough and press it into the bottom of an egg tart mold (see Notes), making sure there is a little extra hanging over the edges. Fill the pastries with as much filling as possible, then grab another portion of dough, flattening it out into a disc using your hands and place it on top of the pie, pinching to seal the edges together. You can then run your fingers across the circumference of the mold to "cut" the excess dough. Repeat with the remaining dough and filling, forming 8 small empadinhas. Place the molds on a baking sheet, brush the pies with egg wash, and bake for 45 to 50 minutes, or until golden brown. Let the empadinhas cool slightly before serving.

BOLINHOS DE FEIJOADA
(FEIJOADA CROQUETTES)

1 lb (454 g) leftover Feijoada na Instant Pot (page 82), without the meat

2 cups (480 ml) water

Kosher salt and freshly ground pepper, as desired

1½ cups (210 g) manioc/cassava flour

1 tsp olive oil

6 oz (170 g) slab or thick-cut bacon, cubed

3 cloves garlic, finely minced

1 bunch collard greens, stemmed and thinly sliced

1½ cups (162 g) breadcrumbs

3 eggs, lightly beaten

Vegetable or canola oil, for frying

Dipping sauce or hot sauce, for serving

If you've got leftover Feijoada na Instant Pot (page 82), you gotta make these croquettes! They are absolutely delicious and go great with a caipirinha or an ice-cold beer. Here we use bacon and collard greens to stuff the bolinhos, but you can stuff them with whatever you like, including leftover meat from the feijoada. Serve with a nice dipping sauce or with some good quality hot sauce for those who like a bit of heat.

Add the feijoada and water to a blender and blend until smooth. Transfer to a large Dutch oven or saucepan over medium low heat, and season with salt and pepper. Once steaming, gradually add the manioc/cassava flour until completely incorporated. You might not need the whole amount and should stop adding when the mixture turns into a dough. Cook, stirring, until you can't see any specks of flour. Reserve to cool.

Once slightly cooled, knead gently on the counter until smooth. Reserve while your prepare the filling..

In a skillet over medium-high heat, heat the olive oil and cook the bacon for 3 minutes, or until turning golden but not yet crispy. Add the garlic and cook for 30 seconds, or until fragrant and no longer raw. Stir in the collard greens and cook for 5 to 8 minutes, or until wilted. Season with salt and pepper. Reserve.

Once the feijoada dough has cooled enough to be handled, make the croquettes. Grab enough dough to form a golf ball–sized ball. Make an indentation in the middle with your thumb, opening it up like a bowl. Fill it with the collard greens filling, and then gather the edges to seal it shut, forming the bolinhos (ball or oblong shape).

Arrange the breadcrumbs in a shallow bowl and season with salt. Arrange the eggs in another bowl. Dip the croquettes in the eggs, letting the excess drip off before coating them in the breadcrumbs.

Heat 3 inches (8 cm) of vegetable oil in a large pot. Once a deep-frying thermometer reads 350°F (180°C), fry the bolinhos, working in batches, for 5 minutes, or until golden brown. Place the fried bolinhos on a plate lined with paper towels to soak up the excess grease, and then serve with a dipping sauce or hot sauce.

COXINHAS DE COSTELINHA DE BOI
(SHORT RIB CROQUETTES)

It'll be difficult to find a Brazilian who doesn't love coxinhas! This version, which uses braised short ribs instead of chicken, is a twist on the traditional and—I dare say—it's impossible to resist! My recipe uses an Instant Pot to make the filling because it cooks the short ribs much faster but you can also cook them on the stove for 3+ hours until they are easily shredded.

FOR THE RIBS

8 oz (226 g) boneless short ribs, cut into 2" (5-cm) chunks

Kosher salt and freshly ground black pepper, as desired

2 tsp (10 ml) vegetable oil, plus more as needed

1 small onion, finely chopped

1 Roma tomato, finely chopped

3 cloves garlic, finely minced

⅓ cup (80 ml) red wine

1 tbsp (16 g) tomato paste

2 cups (480 ml) beef broth

1 tbsp (4 g) chopped parsley

4 oz (113 g) catupiry or cream cheese

FOR THE DOUGH

½ cup (120 ml) of cooking liquid from short ribs

1½ cups (360 ml) beef broth

2 tsp (10 g) kosher salt, divided

1 tbsp (14 g) unsalted butter

2 cups (250 g) all-purpose flour

1 cup (108 g) plain breadcrumbs

3 large eggs

Vegetable or canola oil, for frying

Hot sauce, for serving

To make the short ribs, season them generously with salt and pepper. Set the Instant Pot to sauté mode, heat the oil and brown the short ribs chunks on all sides, 3 minutes per side. Remove to a plate and reserve. Add more oil if needed, and sauté the onion for 2 to 3 minutes, or until translucent. Add the tomato and cook for 3 to 5 minutes, or until softened. Stir in the garlic and cook for 30 seconds, or until fragrant and no longer raw.

Pour in the wine and deglaze the pot, scrubbing all the browned bits from the bottom with a wooden spoon. Cook for 3 to 5 minutes, or until evaporated, and then stir in the tomato paste, cooking for 1 to 2 minutes, or until its color deepens. Stir in the beef broth and return the short ribs to the pot, along with any juices that have collected on the plate. Season with a pinch of salt and pepper, close the pot and cook on high pressure for 45 minutes, with a 10-minute natural pressure release. Remove the short ribs to a plate and shred with two forks. Drain the liquid into a bowl, reserving for later. Return the solids from the strainer to the pot and mix in the shredded beef. Stir in the parsley and cream cheese. Taste for seasoning and adjust as needed.

To make the dough, in a large saucepan, add the reserved liquid, beef broth, 1 teaspoon of the salt and the butter. Bring it to a boil over medium-high heat, and then add all the flour at once. Reduce the heat to low and stir, kneading with the aid of a wooden spoon, until smooth and no longer sticking to the pan. Remove the dough to a lightly oiled counter and let it cool just until you can handle it, then lightly knead until you have a smooth dough.

To assemble the coxinhas, get a tablespoon of dough and shape it into a ball. Then, use your fingers to press the dough, making a little bowl. Stuff the center of the bowl with 2 teaspoons (10 g) of the short rib filling, then gather the top edges to seal, forming a tear-shaped croquette. Repeat with the remaining dough and filling. Place the breadcrumbs in a bowl and season with the remaining salt. In another bowl, lightly beat the eggs. Dip each coxinha in the eggs, and then coat in the breadcrumbs. Reserve. Heat 3 inches (8 cm) of vegetable oil in a large pot. Once a deep-frying thermometer reads 350°F (180°C) degrees, fry the coxinhas, working in batches, for 6 to 8 minutes, or until golden brown on all sides. Remove the coxinhas from the oil with a slotted spoon and transfer to a baking sheet lined with paper towels. Serve immediately with the hot sauce!

FOR THE SAUSAGE

1 tsp olive oil

8 oz (226 g) ground mild sausage

1 medium onion, finely chopped

2 cloves garlic, minced

Kosher salt and freshly ground pepper, as desired

¼ tsp crushed red pepper flakes

¼ tsp allspice

⅓ cup (45 g) toasted pine nuts

FOR THE DOUGH

1½ cups (270 g) fine bulgur wheat (see Notes)

2 cups (480 ml) hot water

1 large onion, peeled and quartered

½ cup (46 g) mint leaves

2 lb (907 g) ground mild sausage

1½ tsp (7 g) kosher salt

½ tsp ground black pepper

¼ tsp allspice

¼ tsp crushed fennel seeds

Vegetable or canola oil, for frying

KIBE DE L'NGUIÇA
(SAUSAGE KIBBEH)

Here's a kibe version you won't find anywhere in the Middle East, since the Islamic and Jewish communities don't eat pork. That being said, if pork is not an issue for you, I highly recommend you give this sausage kibbeh a try, as these are absolutely delicious and a great finger food for parties or game day!

Like most Brazilian deep-fried snacks, these freeze well and can be fried straight from the freezer. So go ahead and make a few batches to freeze. That way you can always have some on hand for when you need to feed a crowd!

To make the filling, in a large skillet over medium-high heat, add the oil. Once the oil is hot, add the sausage and cook, crumbling it into smaller pieces with a wooden spoon, for 5 to 8 minutes, or until browned. Remove with a slotted spoon and reserve. Stir in the onion and cook for 2 to 3 minutes, or until translucent. Add the garlic and cook for 30 seconds, or until fragrant and no longer raw. Return the sausage to the skillet, season with salt and pepper and stir in the red pepper flakes, allspice and pine nuts. Reserve.

To make the dough, in a large bowl, add the bulgur wheat and cover with the hot water. Let it sit for 30 minutes (see Notes), and then drain the water through a strainer, squeezing the wheat to get rid of excess water. In the bowl of a food processor, combine the soaked bulgur wheat, the onion and the mint leaves. Process on high until almost pureed, and then add the ground sausage, salt, pepper, allspice and fennel. Process to a smooth paste.

To form the croquettes, with wet hands, form a golf-sized ball of the dough. Using your index finger, poke a hole in the center of the ball, rotating the dough to make a bowl. Place 2 teaspoons (10 g) of the filling in the center of the bowl, and then gather the edges together to seal, shaping the croquette like a football. Repeat with the remaining dough to make 30 croquettes.

Heat 3 inches (8 cm) of vegetable oil in a large Dutch oven or a deep fryer. Once a deep-frying thermometer reads 350°F (180°C) degrees, fry the kibbeh, working in batches, for 5 minutes, or until golden brown on all sides. Remove the kibbeh from the oil with a slotted spoon and transfer to a plate lined with paper towels. Serve immediately

NOTES
You can also soak the bulgur wheat overnight in cold water if you prefer.

FOR THE JAM

2 red chile peppers, cored, seeded and finely chopped (see Notes)

1 cup (200 g) granulated sugar

1 large apple, with skin, coarsely grated

½ cup (120 ml) water

Juice of 1 lime

1 cinnamon stick

FOR THE DADINHOS

2 cups (240 g) granulated tapioca (see Notes)

3 cups (335 g) shredded queijo coalho (Halloumi or queso de freir work too)

Kosher salt and freshly ground pink pepper, as desired (see Notes)

1 qt (960 ml) whole milk

Vegetable oil, for frying

DADINHOS DE TAPIOCA COM GELÉIA DE PIMENTA
(FRIED TAPIOCA DICE WITH CHILE PEPPER JAM)

This deep-fried snack features tapioca and queijo coalho! When done right, they are beautifully crispy on the outside and tender and chewy inside. Extremely addictive! The dadinhos are very easy to make, but they do require an evening in the fridge to set before you can cut and fry them. But that's okay, since that will give you plenty of time to make the mandatory accompaniment: a chile pepper jam that will have your taste buds dancing in delight!

To make the jam: In a saucepan, combine the chile peppers, sugar, apple, water, lime juice and cinnamon stick. Cook over medium-low heat for 20 minutes, or until it thickens slightly. Let it cool to thicken further, and then refrigerate for up to 2 weeks.

To make the dadinhos: In a large bowl, combine the tapioca, cheese, salt and pepper. Heat the milk in a saucepan over medium heat until steaming. Pour the milk into the tapioca mixture and whisk it constantly until the cheese melts and the mixture turns into a thick batter.

Line a 9 x 9-inch (23 x 23-cm) pan with parchment paper or plastic wrap, making sure there's an overhang on the sides that will help you lift the cooled dough later. Alternatively, you can use a silicone pan without the need to line it with paper. Pour the batter into the pan, cover with plastic wrap, and then let it cool completely and refrigerate overnight, or until set. Remove the tapioca dough from the pan, trim the sides and cut it into 1 x 1-inch (2.5 x 2.5-cm) cubes.

Heat 3 inches (8 cm) of vegetable oil in a large pot or Dutch oven. Once a deep-frying thermometer reads 350°F (180°C) degrees, fry the dadinhos, working in batches, for 5 minutes, or until golden brown. Remove the dadinhos from the oil with a slotted spoon and transfer to a cooling rack lined with paper towels. Serve immediately with the chile pepper jam!

NOTES

- If you like spicy, keep the seeds of the chile peppers.
- Be careful when buying the tapioca. You want to buy the granulated version, sometimes called instant tapioca, and not the tapioca flour or starch. Tapioca flour is pure tapioca starch and won't work in this recipe.
- If you can't find pink pepper, black or white pepper can be used instead.

BISCOITOS DE POLVILHO
(PARMESAN TAPIOCA COOKIES)

1¾ cups (280 g) polvilho azedo (sour tapioca/manioc starch) (see Notes)

1½ tsp (7 g) kosher salt

½ cup (120 ml) whole milk

½ cup (120 ml vegetable oil

1 large egg

¼ cup (25 g) freshly grated Parmesan cheese

⅔ cup (160 ml) cold water

These are naturally gluten-free Brazilian cookies, which can be sweet or savory. This savory version uses Parmesan cheese to flavor the cookies, creating an irresistible snack.

For this recipe, I highly recommend going the extra mile to find the sour tapioca/manioc starch or ordering it online. You can use regular tapioca flour (which Brazilians call polvilho doce or sweet manioc starch), but the results are not quite the same.

Line four large baking sheets with parchment paper. Preheat the oven to 350°F (180°C).

Combine the polvilho azedo and salt in the bowl of a stand mixer fitted with the paddle attachment. Reserve. In a saucepan over medium heat, add the milk and oil. Heat until it starts to steam. Pour the hot liquid into the starch in the stand mixer, and then turn the mixer to medium speed to combine. It will look grainy and weird, but that's okay. Add the egg and mix, and then add the Parmesan. Once incorporated, slowly add the water, letting the machine mix until the mixture is smooth.

Transfer the batter to a piping bag, and then cut a little bit of the bottom so you can pipe the biscoitos. How much you will cut will depend on how big you'd like your biscoitos. I like mine small, so I cut ½ inch (1.3 cm) off. Pipe the biscoitos onto the prepared baking sheets. Again, size will vary, but I pipe 2-inch (5-cm)-long sticks. You can also pipe them into circles. Bake for 18 to 20 minutes, or until they begin to turn golden brown, turning the sheets halfway through (see Notes). Let them cool completely before serving. Biscoitos de polvilho are best enjoyed the day they are made, but they will keep in an airtight container, at room temperature, for a week. They will lose their crunch with time.

NOTES

- *Polvilho is the same as tapioca starch. It is not cassava starch or flour, which is extracted from cassava root. There are two kinds of polvilho: polvilho doce (which is the tapioca flour/starch widely available here in the U.S.) and polvilho azedo (sour tapioca starch). Unfortunately, you won't find polvilho azedo at your local grocery store here in the States, so you will need to go to a Brazilian store or order it online.*

- *Keep an eye on your biscoitos in the oven, especially when making them for the first time. Don't take them out too early, or they'll be chewy. And don't let them brown too much, or they'll be hard. Once they start turning golden brown, it is time to remove them from the oven!*

1 lb (454 g) pork belly, skin attached, cut into 1" (2.5-cm) cubes

Kosher salt, as desired

Vegetable oil, for frying (see Notes)

Lime wedges, for serving

TORRESMO
(PORK CRACKLING)

Torresmo is the ultimate bar snack! Nothing like crispy, deep-fried pieces of pork belly to go with a cold beer, amirite? Making torresmo is very rewarding but can be messy and even a little dangerous as pork belly can splatter quite a bit while frying. Make sure you use a pot that has a lid, as you'll keep the lid on (but cracked) when the pork is frying to minimize the mess. I also highly recommend you use long kitchen mitts (or wear long sleeves) to protect your skin. Just be very careful when you stir the pot, but know that a few splatters are inevitable!

Season the pork belly cubes generously with salt. Pour 2 inches (5 cm) of oil in a large Dutch oven, then stir in the pork belly. Turn the heat to medium-low, then place the lid on, slightly cracked, to prevent any messes or accidents. Cook for 30 minutes, stirring occasionally. While the pork cooks, you will hear it popping, like popcorn. That is normal! However, you should be very careful every time you open the lid to stir, so you don't burn yourself. After 30 minutes, the torresmo should have stopped popping and is probably already golden brown. Crank the heat up to medium-high and cook, uncovered, for 3 to 5 minutes, or until crispy. Remove the torresmo with a slotted spoon onto a paper towel-lined plate. Serve while still hot with the lime wedges!

NOTES

Some people like to use lard instead of oil to make torresmo. If you want to do that, first melt the lard in the pot before adding the pork belly.

FOR THE DOUGH

3 cups (375 g) all-purpose flour

1 tbsp (18 g) kosher salt

1 cup (240 ml) warm water

1 tbsp (15 ml) vegetable oil

1 tbsp (15 ml) white wine vinegar

1 tbsp (15 ml) cachaça or vodka

Vegetable oil, for frying

FOR THE FILLING

1 lb (454 g) desalted cod (see page 92 for desalting instructions)

¼ cup (60 ml) olive oil

1 onion, finely chopped

2 Roma tomatoes, seeded and cored, finely chopped

2 cloves garlic, minced

½ cup (90 g) finely chopped pitted green olives

2 tbsp (30 ml) water

1 tbsp (8 g) all-purpose flour

2 tbsp (8 g) chopped parsley

Hot sauce, for serving

PASTEL DE BACALHAU
(FRIED COD EMPANADAS)

Pastel is Brazil's most popular street food. In this version, crispy, deep-fried pastéis (pastries) are filled with a savory cod mixture that will have you licking your fingers clean! While you can make this recipe using store-bought empanada dough, I highly recommend you make the dough yourself. It's pretty much foolproof and easy to handle, plus it will produce perfectly light and crunchy pastéis that will rival any pastel de feira (Brazilian empanadas) you would get in Brazil!

To make the dough, in a large bowl, combine the flour and salt. Make a hole in the middle and pour in the water, oil, vinegar and cachaça. Mix well with your hands until it comes together. Transfer to a lightly floured surface and knead until the dough is smooth, elastic and no longer sticking to your hands or counter. Cover with a towel and let it rest for 30 minutes.

To make the filling, bring a large pot of water to a boil, and then add the cod pieces. Cook for 2 to 3 minutes, and then drain. Once the cod is cool enough to handle, use your hands to shred into smaller pieces. Reserve.

In a large skillet over medium heat, heat the olive oil. Add the onion and sauté for 2 to 3 minutes, or until translucent. Add the tomatoes and cook for 3 to 5 minutes, or until they've softened. Stir in the garlic and cook for 30 seconds, or until fragrant and no longer raw. Add the cod and olives.

In a bowl, combine the water and flour, and then pour this mixture into the skillet. Cook for 7 to 8 minutes, or until thickened, and then stir in the parsley.

To assemble the pastéis, divide the dough in half, then roll each one on a floured surface, as thin as you can into a 9 x 12–inch (23 x 30–cm) rectangle. Using a round cookie cutter (I use a 4-inch [10-cm]), cut 15 dough circles out of each dough half and reserve on a baking sheet lined with parchment paper. Alternatively, you can also cut the dough into rectangles as small or big as you'd like. Place a couple of tablespoons of the filling on each circle and then fold into a semicircle, pressing the edges shut. Using a fork, pinch the edges together all around. Heat 3 inches (8 cm) of vegetable oil in a large pot or Dutch oven. Once a deep-frying thermometer reads 350°F (180°C) degrees, fry the pastéis for 2 minutes per side, or until crispy and golden brown. Remove from the oil with a slotted spoon and transfer to a plate lined with paper towels. Serve immediately with the hot sauce!

1 large Yukon Gold potato, peeled

¾ cup (180 ml) lukewarm whole milk

1½ tbsp (23 g) granulated sugar

1½ tsp (6 g) active dry yeast

3¼ cups (406 g) all-purpose flour

1½ tsp (7 g) kosher salt

1 large egg

3 tbsp (42 g) unsalted butter, softened

1 (8.8-oz [250 g]) container catupiry cheese or cream cheese

Egg wash (1 egg beaten with 1 tbsp [15 ml] water)

PÃO DE BATATA
(POTATO ROLLS STUFFED WITH CREAM CHEESE)

This is another one of Brazil's most popular snacks! Just walk in any Brazilian bakery (or school cafeteria), and you'll find these delicious, fluffy potato rolls stuffed with creamy cheese. The good news is that these are easy to make at home, and you can even use cream cheese if you can't find any catupiry. And while these rolls are served as a snack in Brazil, I think they will look (and taste) great as dinner rolls at your holiday table or next dinner party!

Place the potato in a saucepan and cover with water. Cook over medium-high heat until it comes to a boil, then lower the heat to medium-low and cook for 15 to 20 minutes, or until fork tender. Drain and let it dry for a couple of minutes so the excess water can evaporate. Then, mash it with a fork or potato ricer. Reserve.

In a small bowl, combine the milk, sugar and yeast. Cover with a kitchen towel and let it rest for 10 minutes, or until foamy. Reserve.

In the bowl of a stand mixer, whisk together the flour and salt. With the mixer fitted with the dough hook attachment and running on low, add the yeast mixture, the mashed potato, the egg and the butter. Mix until combined, and then increase the speed to medium-high and let the machine knead the dough for 5 to 10 minutes, or until smooth. Transfer the dough to an oiled bowl, cover with a towel and let it proof for 1 hour at room temperature. You can also cold proof it in the fridge overnight.

Punch the dough and divide it into 12 equal parts. Form each part into a ball, and then flatten them into circles. Place a dollop of the catupiry in the center of each dough, and then gather the edges up to seal. Roll the stuffed dough on the counter to shape it into a ball, and then place on a baking sheet lined with parchment paper, arranging the balls with 2 inches (5 cm) of space between them. Cover with a damp towel and let them proof for 45 minutes to 1 hour, or until puffed and almost doubled in size again.

Preheat the oven to 350°F (180°C).

Brush the rolls with the egg wash and bake for 30 to 35 minutes, or until golden brown. Remove from the oven and let them cool before serving.

1 cup (240 ml) lukewarm water

2 tsp (8 g) active dry yeast

1 tbsp (15 ml) olive oil, plus more as needed

3 cups (411 g) bread flour

1½ tsp (7 g) kosher salt

1 lb (454 g) Calabresa sausage, thinly sliced (see Notes)

¼ cup (25 g) freshly grated Parmesan cheese

NOTES

You'll want to slice the Calabresa as thinly as possible. You can do this by hand using a sharp chef's knife or using the food processor. A good tip is to freeze the sausages for 20 to 30 minutes to firm them up, which will make it easier to slice them!

PÃO DE CALABRESA
(SAUSAGE BREAD)

You won't find a pizzeria in all of São Paulo that doesn't serve pão de Calabresa (Calabresa bread), sometimes called tortano de Calabresa. It is almost a Paulista tradition to have some while waiting for your pizza to be ready! And while this recipe makes a classic (plain) Calabresa bread, you can customize it by adding whatever ingredients you love, such as cheese, sliced onions, olives or even some roasted garlic.

In a small bowl, combine the water and yeast. Cover with a towel and let it sit for 10 minutes to proof. If, after 10 minutes, your yeast is foaming up, it is active and ready to be used. Stir in the olive oil and reserve.

In the bowl of a stand mixer fitted with the dough hook attachment, add the flour and salt. With the mixer running on low, gradually pour in the yeast mixture. Let the machine work to combine all the ingredients into a dough. Once a dough has formed, increase the speed to medium-high and let the mixer knead the dough for 3 minutes. Turn the mixer off, cover the bowl with a kitchen towel, and let it rest for 15 minutes.

Once rested, knead on medium-high again for 3 minutes. Divide the dough into two equal parts, and then transfer to two oiled bowls. Cover with greased plastic wrap and let it rise for 8 to 24 hours in the fridge (or up to 3 hours at room temperature), or until doubled in size.

Roll each piece of dough on a lightly floured surface to form two 13 x 10-inch (33 x 25-cm) rectangles, leaving a ½-inch (1.3-cm) border all around. Arrange the Calabresa on top of each rolled dough, drizzle some olive oil, and then slowly roll each into a tight 13-inch (33-cm) log, pinching the ends to seal it shut. Braid the dough loosely to form one loaf. Transfer to a loaf pan, cover with a damp towel and let it rise for 1 hour, or until puffy.

Preheat the oven to 400°F (200°C).

Brush the loaf generously with olive oil, and then sprinkle the Parmesan on top. Cover with foil and bake for 20 minutes. Remove the foil and bake for 25 to 30 minutes, or until golden brown on top. A cooked loaf should hit 200°F (95°C) when a thermometer is stuck into its thickest part. Remove the loaf from the oven and let it cool in the pan for 20 minutes before carefully taking it out of the pan to a cooling rack. Let it cool to room temperature before serving. (It is important to let the bread cool to room temperature as it will continue cooking as it cools.) That being said, if desired, you can then rewarm it to serve!

2 large sweet onions, thinly sliced into rounds (see Notes)

1½ cups (360 ml) extra virgin olive oil

2 tbsp (30 ml) cachaça

¼ cup (60 ml) water

Kosher salt and freshly ground pepper, as desired

1 tsp dried oregano

VINAGRETE DE CEBOLA NA CACHAÇA
(CACHAÇA PICKLED ONIONS)

When I was growing up, my parents used to take us to an Italian cantina in São Paulo that served a version of these pickled onions. I don't remember any other dishes from that restaurant, but the onions will be forever in my mind because we always ordered them!

If you love onions, this is a great relish to serve with grilled meat or even burgers and hot dogs, but it can also substitute for the classic vinaigrette that Brazilians often eat with feijoada (page 82) and other bean dishes. Or you can do like I do and devour at least some of them straight out of the bowl with some crusty bread.

Place the onion rounds in a bowl of ice water and let them soak for 15 minutes (see Notes). Drain, then transfer the onions to a large bowl. Pour in the olive oil, cachaça and water. Season generously with salt and pepper, then stir in the oregano. Taste and adjust seasoning as needed. Cover and refrigerate for at least 2 hours or up to 3 weeks.

NOTES
Soaking the onions in cold water for 15 minutes will soften the flavor, mellowing their bite out a bit.

SOBReMESA

DESSERTS AND TREATS

Brazilian desserts are so special that, in my opinion, they deserve a book of their own. For us Brazilians, a meal simply is not complete without our beloved sobremesa!

This chapter features not only desserts, such as my grandma's famous Pavê da Manuda (Manuda's Trifle; page 140) and Mousse de Maracujá com Chocolate (Passion Fruit Mousse with Chocolate; page 128), but also sweet treats that are meant to be enjoyed as afternoon snacks, accompanied by our cafézinho (coffee) or some tea.

If you are ready to dive into the world of Brazilian sweets, make sure to grab several cans of sweetened condensed milk on your next grocery store run, as you will find that it is a recurring ingredient in lots of these recipes. We Brazilians simply love our leite condensado!

1 (14-oz [396-g]) can sweetened condensed milk

1 cup (93 g) shredded coconut

1 tbsp (14 g) unsalted butter, plus more as needed

1½ cups (300 g) granulated sugar

¾ cups (180 ml) water

1½ tbsp (23 ml) white wine vinegar

BALA DE VIDRO
(COCONUT CANDY)

Bala de vidro, also known as bala baiana, is the Brazilian adaptation of the Portuguese bala de ovo. While the Portuguese use egg yolks to make the candies, Brazilians like to use sweetened condensed milk instead. The creamy, irresistible coconut filling is prepared like a brigadeiro. Once it's set, it is shaped into balls and coated in hard, crack-stage caramel, creating the glass effect that gives them their name!

Make sure to let the candies cool and dry completely before enjoying. You want their exterior to snap when bitten into, which won't happen if they are still soft, and the caramel will stick to your teeth.

In a large saucepan or small Dutch oven, add the condensed milk, coconut and butter. Cook over medium-low heat for 10 minutes, or until it thickens and the mixture starts releasing from the bottom of the pan. That will happen at 190°F (88°C), if you prefer to use a thermometer. Transfer the mixture to a plate that has been generously greased with butter, spreading it into a single layer. Cover with plastic wrap and let it cool completely. Once the coconut mixture has cooled, grease your hands with a little butter and form balls with 1 tablespoon (15 g) of dough per ball. Reserve at room temperature.

In another saucepan, mix the sugar, water and vinegar. Cook over medium heat, stirring often, until the sugar has dissolved. Stop stirring and let the mixture boil—untouched—until it caramelizes and turns a beautiful amber color. It is okay to gently swirl the pan as needed. We want the caramel to reach the hard-crack stage, which happens at 300 to 310°F (150 to 154°C), so I highly recommend using a kitchen thermometer to check. Once at the hard-crack stage, remove the caramel from the stove.

With a fork or dipping tool, start dipping the coconut balls in the caramel, one at a time, letting the excess drip before placing them on a plate or baking sheet lined with parchment paper. Let the candies set until the caramel hardens completely, and then serve. The candies will keep at room temperature for 3 to 4 days. You can wrap them individually in cellophane wrappers if you wish to give them as gifts.

10 paçocas (260 g), divided (see Notes)

1 (14-oz [396-g]) can sweetened condensed milk

2 tbsp (32 g) creamy peanut butter

¼ tsp kosher salt

2 cups (480 ml) heavy cream, cold

SORVETE DE PAÇOCA
(BRAZILIAN PEANUT CANDY ICE CREAM)

Paçoca is a traditional Brazilian treat made of peanuts. It is especially enjoyed during our winter festivities (festas juninas), which happen during the month of June. These treats are delicious—and incredibly addictive—as they are, but I thought it'd be fun to transform them into ice cream. And, boy, are you in for a treat! This ice cream is rich, creamy and bursting with peanut flavor. The perfect treat for peanut lovers!

Gently crush the paçocas by hand. Reserve. (You will need half for the ice cream base mixture and half to add as a mix-in at the end of the churning process.)

In a medium bowl, combine the condensed milk, peanut butter, salt, heavy cream and half of the crushed paçocas. Whisk until well incorporated. Pour the mixture into your ice cream maker and churn for 25 to 30 minutes, or according to the manufacturer's directions. Depending on your machine, you will get a signal when it's time to add any mix-ins, which are the remaining paçocas. If your machine doesn't have this feature, just pay attention and add it once the motor starts slowing down and the ice cream has solidified but is not yet completely churned. Once you've added the remaining crushed paçocas, continue churning until it reaches a soft ice cream consistency. You can serve the ice cream right away, if you like it on the softer side, or freeze it to harden further. It will keep for up to 2 weeks if stored in an airtight container.

NOTES

* In the U.S., you can find paçocas in Brazilian grocery stores or online. If you are not able to find them, I have a recipe for homemade ones on my website.

* If you don't own an ice cream machine, don't worry! You can still make this recipe. Just whip the heavy cream until stiff peaks form before folding it into the sweetened condensed milk mixture. Then, transfer to a freezer-safe container and carefully swirl in the remaining half of the paçocas. Cover with plastic wrap and freeze until firm!

⅔ cup (150 g) unsalted butter, softened

2 cups + 2 tbsp (266 g) all-purpose flour

½ cup (100 g) granulated sugar

1 large egg

6.5 oz (188 g) guava paste

Confectioner's sugar for sprinkling

BELISCÃO DE GOIABADA
(GUAVA PASTE PINCH COOKIES)

These guava paste-filled cookies might look simple, but they are absolutely addictive! So much so that I feel I must warn you that you will probably devour a whole batch by yourself without even noticing. Ask me how I know . . .

The buttery cookies melt in your mouth while depositing the sweet and slightly floral guava paste on your taste buds, making them tingle all over with excitement! These taste best the day they were made, but they will keep for up to a week when stored in an airtight container at room temperature. That being said, I highly doubt they will last that long!

In a large bowl, combine the butter, flour, sugar and egg. Use your hands to mix everything together until a dough forms. Divide the dough into two equal parts and form each part into a disc. Working with one disc at a time, place the disc between two sheets of parchment paper and roll it ¼-inch (6-mm)-thick. Cut into rounds with a 1½-inch (4-cm) round cutter. Repeat with the second dough disc. You can gather the scraps and re-roll to form more cookies.

Cut the guava paste into 1-inch (2.5-cm)-long strips that are ¼ inch (6 mm) thick. If you're having difficulty slicing the guava paste, a good trick is to pop it in the freezer for 10 minutes. Place the guava paste strips in the center of each round cookie dough. Then, gather the ends of each cookie and bring them together, pinching them to seal. Transfer the cookies to 1 to 2 parchment paper-lined baking sheets, and then place in the freezer for 10 to 15 minutes.

Preheat the oven to 350°F (180°C) while the cookies are in the freezer.

Bake the cookies for 15 to 18 minutes, or until beginning to turn golden. Remove from oven and let them cool, then sprinkle with confectioner's sugar before serving.

FOR THE MOUSSE

1½ tsp (5 g) unflavored gelatin

3 tbsp (45 ml) cold water

1 (14-oz [396-g]) can sweetened condensed milk

1½ cups (290 g) passion fruit pulp, no seeds (see Notes)

1 cup (240 ml) heavy cream

FOR THE GANACHE

1¼ cups (300 ml) heavy cream

7 oz (198 g) chopped bittersweet chocolate (see Notes)

¼ tsp kosher salt

½ tsp pure vanilla extract

Chocolate shavings, for garnishing

MOUSSE DE MARACUJÁ COM GANACHE DE CHOCOLATE

(PASSION FRUIT MOUSSE WITH CHOCOLATE GANACHE)

Mousse de maracujá is perhaps Brazil's most popular dessert. This version, which is topped with a delicious and rich ganache, takes this beloved dessert to a whole new level! The bittersweet chocolate ganache pairs amazingly with the creamy, tangy passion fruit mousse, providing an interesting contrast.

The hardest part of this recipe will be having to wait for it to set in the fridge, twice! And while you can dig into it as soon as the ganache has set, I recommend letting it hang out at room temperature for 10 to 20 minutes before serving so the ganache can soften a bit, making it easier to cut through with a spoon.

To make the mousse, in a small bowl, stir the gelatin into the cold water. Microwave for 25 to 40 seconds, or until dissolved. Reserve until it cools.

In a blender, combine the condensed milk, passion fruit pulp, heavy cream and the dissolved gelatin. Blend on high speed for 3 to 5 minutes, or until smooth and slightly thickened. Transfer the mousse to a large serving dish or to individual dessert cups. Refrigerate for 4 hours, or until it sets.

To make the ganache, place the heavy cream in a saucepan and heat over medium heat until steaming. Place the chocolate in a bowl and pour in the hot cream. Let it stand for 1 to 2 minutes, and then stir until the chocolate completely dissolves. Stir in the salt and vanilla. Pour the ganache over the set mousse, and refrigerate for 2 to 4 hours or overnight, or until it sets. Decorate with chocolate shavings before serving.

NOTES
- *While you can definitely make this recipe with fresh passion fruit, you will probably have better luck finding it in frozen puree form. Just thaw it and use as directed.*
- *Chocolate chips can be used if they are good quality, such as Callebaut®. Otherwise, just choose a nice chocolate bar and use that instead.*

YIELD: 25 BRIGADEIROS

2 tbsp (28 g) unsalted butter, plus extra as needed

1 (14-oz [396-g]) can sweetened condensed milk

1 cup (168 g) semisweet Belgian chocolate, such as Callebaut chocolate chips

¼ tsp kosher salt

Chocolate sprinkles, for rolling

BRIGADEIRO DE CHOCOLATE BELGA

(BELGIAN CHOCOLATE BRIGADEIRO)

Brigadeiros have a special place in every Brazilian's heart. They are a must-have at special celebrations, from kids' parties to weddings, but they are also part of everyday life, enjoyed as a treat at a brigadeiria or coffee shop to soothe a sweet tooth or as a pick-me-up in the middle of a difficult day.

While the classic recipe is made with cocoa powder, this version, which is sometimes called brigadeiro gourmet, uses high-quality Belgian chocolate instead.

Brush a large plate generously with melted butter and reserve.

In a large saucepan or small Dutch oven, combine the condensed milk, butter, chocolate and salt. Cook over medium-low heat, stirring constantly, for 10 minutes, or until the mixture thickens. You'll be able to tell it's ready when it starts pulling away from the sides of the pot. If you prefer to use a kitchen thermometer, the brigadeiro is done at 200 to 210°F (95 to 99°C).

Transfer the brigadeiro to the buttered plate, cover with plastic wrap and let it cool to room temperature. Then, place in the fridge for 30 to 60 minutes so it firms up a bit more. Once the brigadeiro is firm, spread the chocolate sprinkles on a plate. Rub a little butter on your hands and roll the brigadeiro into balls. Sizes vary, and it is up to personal preference, but I use a little less than a tablespoon to make 25 small balls. Roll the balls in the sprinkles until completely covered, and then place them on a serving platter or—if you have them—in individual candy cups. The brigadeiros will keep at room temperature, stored in an airtight container, for 2 to 3 days. Alternatively, they can be refrigerated for 1 to 2 weeks.

2 tbsp (28 g) unsalted butter, softened, plus extra as needed

2 (14-oz [396-g]) cans sweetened condensed milk

¼ cup (60 ml) heavy cream

¼ tsp kosher salt

¼ cup (22 g) cocoa powder

1½ cups (156 g) hand-crushed graham crackers (from 10 graham cracker sheets) (see Notes)

1 cup (200 g) sugar, for rolling

PALHA ITALIANA
(BRAZILIAN CHOCOLATE AND COOKIE FUDGE)

Despite the name, which translates to "Italian straw" in English, this is a treat that is 100-percent Brazilian. It's inspired by the Italian salami di cioccolato (chocolate salami), but is softer, like a fudge. This treat is traditionally made with store-bought maizena cookies, which you can find online or at Brazilian grocery stores, but I find that it works just as well with widely available graham crackers.

After the fudge has cooled and set, it should be cut into squares (as big or as small as you want) and rolled in sugar. You can use either granulated sugar (my choice) or powdered sugar, depending on the desired aesthetics.

Brush an 8 x 8-inch (20 x 20–cm) pan generously with butter. Alternatively, you can use a silicone pan, which you wouldn't need to grease.

In a Dutch oven or heavy-bottomed pot, combine the butter, condensed milk, heavy cream, salt and cocoa powder. Cook over medium-low heat, stirring constantly with a rubber spatula, until it thickens. You will know it is ready when it starts coming off the bottom of the pot, but if you prefer, you can also use a candy thermometer and stop cooking when it reaches 210 to 215°F (99 to 102°C). Turn off the heat and immediately stir in the crushed graham crackers. Pour the fudge into the prepared pan and let it cool to room temperature. Refrigerate for at least 2 hours, and then cut into 12 squares. Roll each fudge into the sugar and serve.

NOTES
When hand crushing the crackers, make sure you are not pulverizing them. You want pieces of the crackers, not crumbs.

⅔ cup (160 ml) water

1½ cups (300 g) sugar

8 large egg yolks, at room temperature

1½ cups (360 ml) coconut milk

BABA DE MOÇA
(BRAZILIAN COCONUT CUSTARD)

Baba de moça is a traditional Brazilian dessert with Portuguese origins, made of egg yolks, sugar and coconut milk. It is cooked until it reaches a spoonable consistency, and it's served as is or used in cakes, tortes and other baked goods.

While the recipe calls for very few ingredients, it can be temperamental and requires you cook it just right to achieve the perfect consistency. Because of that, I highly recommend using a thermometer instead of just playing the guessing game when determining if it is done. Finally, it is not traditional, but I sometimes like to add a few drops of vanilla extract or orange blossom water to the custard to give it some depth of flavor!

In a saucepan, combine the water and sugar and cook over medium-low heat. You can stir it at the beginning to help the sugar dissolve, but once it's dissolved, you shouldn't touch it anymore. Let it boil until it reaches the thread stage at 225°F (110°C). If you don't own a thermometer, just take a small amount of the syrup onto a spoon, and let it drip into the pan. It should spin a long thread.

In a bowl, whisk together the egg yolks and coconut milk. Slowly pour the sugar syrup into the yolk mixture, whisking constantly, to temper the eggs. The resulting mixture should be smooth, without any pieces of scrambled eggs. Transfer the custard to the saucepan and cook, over medium-low heat, whisking constantly, for 15 to 20 minutes, or until it thickens. Do not let it boil. The custard is done at 190°F (88°C). If you're using it as a filling for cakes and baked goods, cook longer so it thickens to a stiffer consistency. Pour it into individual serving cups or ramekins, or into a bowl if using in another recipe. Cover with plastic wrap, making sure the plastic is touching the custard to prevent the surface from hardening. Let it cool to room temperature, then transfer to the fridge to cool overnight.

½ cup (100 g) granulated sugar

½ cup (120 ml) whole milk

¼ cup (60 ml) melted unsalted butter

1 large egg

1 tbsp (15 ml) apple cider vinegar

1 tbsp (14 g) baking powder

¼ tsp kosher salt

2½ cups (313 g) all-purpose flour

Vegetable oil, for frying

Cinnamon sugar (¼ cup [50 g] sugar mixed with ½ tsp cinnamon)

CUECA VIRADA
(FRIED PASTRIES)

These deep-fried pastries, called cueca virada, crostoli, orelha de gato or cavaquinho, taste just like beignets. They are often served as an afternoon treat along a cup of coffee. The funny name comes from the pastries being shaped like twisted underwear (briefs), but you'll probably have better luck imagining them like bowties.

The dough will keep in the fridge for up to 3 to 4 days or in the freezer for up to 3 months, so you can shape the cuecas and keep them in the fridge or freezer for when you're craving them. That being said, once you fry them, they are best enjoyed right away

In a large bowl, whisk together the sugar, milk, butter, egg, vinegar, baking powder and salt. Gradually add the flour, 1 cup (125 g) at a time, mixing with a spatula. At the end, it will be hard to mix with the spatula, so switch to your hands, mixing gently to form a dough. Transfer the dough to a lightly floured counter and knead gently, just until it's smooth. You do not want to overwork this dough! Shape into a ball, place in a bowl, cover in plastic wrap and refrigerate for 15 minutes.

Divide the dough in half and, working with one dough at a time while keeping the other covered, roll into a ¼-inch (6-mm)-thick rectangle that's 10 x 8 inches (25 x 20 cm). With a sharp knife or bench scraper, cut the dough into 4 x 2-inch (10 x 5-cm) rectangles. Make a 2-inch (5-cm) slit lengthwise in the center of the rectangles, and then pass one of the ends of the rectangle through the opening, making a cueca. (It will resemble a bow tie shape.) Repeat with the second dough. If you have scraps, you can gather them and re-roll once to make more cuecas.

Heat 3 inches (8 cm) of oil in a large Dutch oven over medium heat until a deep fryer thermometer reads 350°F (180°C). Working in batches, fry the cuecas until puffy and golden brown, flipping them once so they cook on both sides. Transfer the cuecas to a plate lined with paper towels to get rid of any excess grease, and then toss them in the cinnamon sugar while they are still hot. Serve immediately.

2 tbsp (28 g) unsalted butter, softened, plus more for the pan

Granulated sugar, for dusting

2 (14-oz [396-g]) cans sweetened condensed milk

1 cup (240 ml) heavy cream

6 tbsp (32 g) cocoa powder

4 large eggs

2 egg yolks

¼ tsp kosher salt

Chocolate sprinkles, for decorating (optional)

BRIGADEIRÃO
(BRAZILIAN CHOCOLATE FLAN)

Brigadeirão, like the name suggests, is essentially a huge brigadeiro, but in flan form! It's creamy, chocolatey and absolutely irresistible. This dessert is not only crowd-pleasing, but also very easy to make. The batter is mixed in the blender, and then cooked in the oven in a water bath, until just set. Garnishing with sprinkles is optional, but highly recommended.

Preheat the oven to 325°F (160°C). Heat a kettle or pot of water for the water bath. Brush a 9½-inch (24-cm) ring cake pan with butter and dust with granulated sugar. Swirl and tap around until there's an even coat, then discard the excess sugar.

In a blender, combine the condensed milk, heavy cream, cocoa powder, butter, eggs, egg yolks and salt, and blend until smooth. Pour this into the prepared pan, and then cover the pan with foil and place in a roasting pan or baking dish that is large enough to accommodate it. Carefully pour the hot water into the roasting pan. The water should reach halfway up the sides of the ring pan. Bake for 50 to 75 minutes, or until the brigadeirão is set but still jiggly in the center. It will continue setting as it cools!

Remove from the oven and let the brigadeirão cool in the water bath. Then, remove the ring pan from the water bath, wipe dry, cover with plastic wrap and refrigerate for at least 4 hours (or overnight).

To unmold, gently run a thin sharp knife around the edges of the pan, including the edges of the middle ring. Invert it onto a serving platter. The flan should come right off, but if it doesn't, let it sit inverted for a couple of minutes to see if it will unmold. If necessary, run the knife around the edges again. Decorate the brigadeirão with chocolate sprinkles (if using), covering the whole top and sides. Then, serve cold!

PAVÊ DA MANUDA

(MANUDA'S TRIFLE)

FOR THE CREAM LAYER

2 (14-oz [396-g]) cans sweetened condensed milk

1 qt (960 ml) whole milk, divided

3 tbsp (24 g) cornstarch

4 egg yolks, at room temperature

FOR THE LADYFINGER LAYER

2 cups (480 ml) whole milk

½ cup (44 g) cocoa powder

1 tsp cognac

20 ladyfinger cookies

FOR THE WHIPPED CREAM LAYER

2½ cups (600 ml) heavy cream

1 cup (120 g) powdered sugar

1 tsp vanilla extract

Grated chocolate, for garnishing

Pavês, in all shapes, flavors and forms, are a big part of Brazilian cuisine. They are homestyle, layered desserts that consist of layers of pastry cream, cookies (usually ladyfingers or maizena cookies) and whipped cream. Like my grandma's Estrogonofe de Carne (Beef Stroganoff; page 11), this recipe has a special place in my heart! I'm sharing it with you with almost no alterations from the original, with the only difference being the fact that I make double the amount of pastry cream than my grandma used to make. Because more pastry cream is always better!

The pavê can be assembled and served as a big tray or as individual portions in dessert cups. And while it can be prepared a day or two in advance, I recommend making and adding the whipped cream the day you plan on serving it, as it will deflate and weep after a day in the fridge.

To make the cream, in a large Dutch oven or heavy-bottomed pot, combine the condensed milk with 3 cups (720 ml) of the whole milk. Cook over medium heat until it begins to steam. While the milk is cooking, whisk the remaining milk, cornstarch and egg yolks in a bowl. Once the milk is steaming, pour a ladleful of the hot liquid into the bowl with the egg yolk mixture, whisking as you pour to temper the eggs. Return this mixture to the pot and cook until the cream thickens. If you want to use a kitchen thermometer to check, the cream is done when it reaches 200°F (95°C). Remove it from heat, let it cool slightly and then pour it into a 9 x 13-inch (23 x 33-cm) baking dish. Reserve to cool.

To make the ladyfinger layer, use the same pot you used for the pastry cream without washing it. Add the milk and cocoa powder and cook over medium heat, whisking, until the cocoa powder dissolves completely and thickens very slightly. Remove from the heat and stir in the cognac. Dip the ladyfingers into the cocoa mixture one at a time, and then arrange them in an even layer over the cream in the baking dish. You might need to break a few to make them fit. Cover the baking dish with plastic wrap and refrigerate overnight.

The next day, make the whipped cream by combining the heavy cream, powdered sugar and vanilla extract in a bowl. Mix with a hand mixer until soft peaks form. Spread the whipped cream onto the ladyfingers layer. Cover and refrigerate, until ready to serve. Right before serving, garnish the pavê by grating some chocolate over the whipped cream.

CHICO BALANCEADO
(LAYERED BANANA DESSERT)

Banana lovers, rejoice! Made with layers of pastry cream, caramelized bananas and toasted Swiss meringue, this dessert is for those who not only love bananas but also have a pronounced sweet tooth, as it is quite indulgent.

Very popular in the south of Brazil, this dessert takes other names as you travel up the country, such as banana na travessa, manézinho araújo, merengue de banana and gato de botas.

FOR THE CREAM LAYER

4 large egg yolks, at room temperature

2 tbsp + 1 tsp (19 g) cornstarch

1 (14-oz [396-g]) can sweetened condensed milk

2 cups (480 ml) whole milk

1 tbsp (15 ml) vanilla extract

½ cup (120 ml) heavy cream

FOR THE BANANAS LAYER

1 cup (200 g) granulated sugar

½ cup (120 ml) hot tap water

7 bananas, peeled and sliced ½"
(1.3-cm) thick

To make the cream layer, in a medium bowl, whisk the egg yolks and cornstarch until combined. Reserve.

In a saucepan, add the condensed milk and whole milk. Heat over medium heat, stirring occasionally so it doesn't burn on the bottom, for 10 minutes, or until steaming and beginning to boil. Add two ladles of the hot milk to the bowl with the yolk cornstarch mixture, whisking to temper the eggs. Pour this tempered mixture into the saucepan with the remaining milk. Lower the heat to medium-low and cook until it thickens, and then cook—stirring constantly—for 3 minutes. Remove from the heat and stir in the vanilla and heavy cream. Pour the pastry cream in a large baking dish. Reserve to cool.

To make the caramelized bananas, heat the sugar in a large skillet or sauté pan over medium-low heat. Once the sugar begins to melt, start stirring often (or swirling the pan) for 4 to 5 minutes, or until the sugar has completely melted and turned an amber color. Do not leave it unattended, or the caramel will burn! Carefully pour in the hot tap water. The caramel will solidify, and that's okay! Cook, stirring or swirling constantly, for 2 minutes, or until it liquifies again. Cook for an additional 2 minutes, or until it thickens slightly. Add the sliced bananas and give it a good stir. Cook for 1 to 2 minutes, or until the bananas begin to soften. Do not overcook or the bananas might fall apart! Turn the heat off and let the caramelized bananas cool down in the skillet for 5 minutes. Then, transfer to the baking dish, gently spreading them on top of the pastry cream. Reserve.

(continued)

FOR THE SWISS MERINGUE LAYER

1 cup (200 g) granulated sugar

¼ tsp kosher salt

4 egg whites

CHICO BALANCEADO
(CONTINUED)

To make the Swiss meringue, add the sugar, salt and egg whites to the bowl of a stand mixer. Fill a saucepan halfway with water and bring it to a boil over medium-high heat. Lower the heat to a simmer and place the stand mixer bowl on top of the steaming saucepan, creating a double boiler. The bottom of the bowl should not touch the water. Cook, stirring continuously, for 6 to 8 minutes, or until the sugar has dissolved and the mixture is warm to the touch. You can check by rubbing it between your fingers—you shouldn't be able to feel any granules of sugar. Attach the bowl to your stand mixer base, fitted with the whisk attachment, and beat on medium-low speed for 2 minutes, or until whites begins to foam. Gradually increase the speed, beating for 15 minutes, or until stiff glossy peaks form and the bowl is no longer warm to the touch. On humid days, it might take longer—up to 20 minutes.

Pipe or spread the meringue on top of the caramelized bananas, creating the final layer of this dessert. If you've chosen to spread instead of pipe, use the back of a spoon to do up and down motions, fluffing the meringue to make decorative peaks. Torch the meringue with a kitchen torch or broil in the oven for a couple of minutes, rotating often, until golden brown. Chill in the fridge for 4 to 6 hours before serving. This dessert is best enjoyed the day it's made. Because it contains meringue, it won't keep more than a couple of days, as the meringue will start weeping. To keep it slightly longer, you can try adding a pinch of cream of tartar when making the meringue.

ACKNOWLEDGMENTS

I would like to start by saying this book would not exist without my grandmother, Manuda, who taught me that feeding people is an act of love. I don't think there'll ever be a day where I don't feel sad that she's not here anymore, but our love is eternal and I am forever grateful for being blessed with her in my life.

A huge thanks to my mom, Regina, who helped me test and perfect some of the recipes in this book. I couldn't do this without her!

I would also like to thank my husband, for giving me daily pep talks and support that helped me overcome my anxiety and self-doubt, and also my two girls, for being cute and providing some much needed comic relief at times.

My dad, José Olavo, also deserves a mention. Since I was a kid, he has made it clear that he would support me no matter what and that I could succeed in whatever I chose to do. And throughout the journey of writing a book, he kept messaging me to remind me that he wanted to buy ten copies. At least I know I will sell at least that many! Thanks, Dad!

Thanks also to my in-laws, Joyce and Neil, for helping with the girls when I needed to test recipes or write; my aunt Renata for always being an inspiration and a third opinion whenever me and my mom disagreed on something related to my grandma's recipes; Miracy for being my source for recipes from the northeast of Brazil; and my cyber friend Izabel Campana (@izacozinha on Instagram) for helping me brainstorm some of these recipes, providing invaluable advice as she's also a Brazilian living abroad.

Finally, my eternal gratitude to Page Street Publishing; my editor, Marissa; and the designers for helping me cross "writing a book" off my bucket list! Since I have already planted a tree, I guess it's now time to figure out how to ride an elephant.

ABOUT THE AUTHOR

Olivia Mesquita is the creator of Olivia's Cuisine, a recipe website that features comfort food dishes from all over the world. Born and raised in São Paulo, Brazil, she inherited her love of homemade food and cooking from her grandmother, Marilda (who was known by all as "Manuda," since Olivia couldn't pronounce "Marilda" when she first learned to speak).

When she moved to New York City in 2010, Olivia encountered a challenge: the ingredients that she would need to make the Brazilian recipes that were near and dear to her heart were not widely available in supermarkets in Manhattan and required a long subway trip to Brazilian stores in Queens or Newark (or her mother smuggling a suitcase full of food through customs every time she came to visit). So she took it upon herself to adapt her family recipes, modifying them so they could be prepared with ingredients that she could find at her local grocery store.

And that's how, in 2014, she founded Olivia's Cuisine, which started as an online food diary but is now her full-time job and career. Her work has been featured in several publications, such as Kitchn (thekitchn.com), *Country Living*, *Parade* and Buzzfeed.

Olivia is currently experiencing the American suburban life, living on the outskirts of New York—a place called New Jersey—and raising her two young girls, Rebecca and Valentina, and her dogs, Lola and Juju (which is short for Julia Child), along with her husband, Tim. On a regular day, you can find her tweaking recipes in the kitchen, photographing dishes in her studio and spending an obscene amount of time engaging with her community on Instagram, Facebook and Pinterest.

INDEX